Snakes Alive

Ted Nicholas

Onwards and Upwards Publishers

Berkeley House, 11 Nightingale Crescent, Leatherhead, Surrey, KT24 6PD.
www.onwardsandupwards.org

Copyright © Ted Nicholas 2012

The right of Ted Nicholas to be identified as the author of this work has been asserted by the author in accordance with the Copyright, Designs and Patents Act 1988.

All rights reserved.

No part of this publication may be reproduced or transmitted in any form or by any means, electronic or mechanical, including photocopy, recording or any information storage and retrieval system, without permission in writing from the author or publisher.

Printed in the UK.

Photographs used by permission.

We thank Oswestry School for their kind permission to reprint the 'Last Day' photograph (p49) from their website (**oswestryschool.org.uk**).

We thank Old Oswestrian for their kind permission to reprint photographs of Oswestry School and its chapel (pp.49-50).

Unless otherwise indicated, scripture quotations are taken from the Holy Bible, King James Version, Cambridge, 1769. Scripture quotations marked (NIV) are taken from the Holy Bible, NEW INTERNATIONAL VERSION © 1978, 1984 by International Bible Society. Used by permission of Hodder & Stoughton. All rights reserved.

Scripture quotations marked (NIV) are taken from the Holy Bible, NEW INTERNATIONAL VERSION © 1978, 1984 by International Bible Society. Used by permission of Hodder & Stoughton. All rights reserved.

ISBN: 978-1-907509-61-2
Cover illustration: Sue Hazeldine, Living Waters Church
Cover layout: Leah-Maarit

Contents

Foreword 5

Preface 7

Introduction 9

1. The Beginning 11
2. Old Marton 27
3. School 37
4. Home 51
5. Sandhurst and India 65
6. Last days in England 77
7. Arrival 87
8. Marriage and Metabeleland 109
9. Farming 115
10. Changing Careers 121
11. Farming in the Lowveld 127
12. Agricultural Finance 135
13. Mashonaland East 143
14. Civil War Years 149
15. Changing Careers Again 157
16. Retirement 163

Last Word 173

Addendum 175

Snakes Alive

Foreword

What an exciting, dangerous and extraordinary life my father has led for more than 85 years. I am delighted to pen this foreword as it gives me opportunity to connect his life with ours as we continue to flow together with understanding and knowledge of our heritage. What changes and advances there have been - from pitching sheaves of corn in the thirties as a teenager to writing his memoirs through a specially designed computer program today - all whilst being registered blind.

As we get older, questions about where we came from and what things were like before our own memories began become important. To members of an immigrant family who have had to keep moving, ideas of identity are tied up in the past. I am very pleased that my father has been able to record for us some of his memories and to describe for the lesser informed what life was like in an England that has now disappeared.

As my father reflects upon the life he lived in his youth, he helps us to understand how it was back then, even though those of us from the younger generation we might have difficulty in relating to the circumstances of his day. In those days young people knew no other way; they had no electricity, no television, no motor car, and yet they grew up as healthy, happy, resourceful youngsters. My father is now nearly ninety and still going strong!

Many of the events described in here about Africa occurred when I was living at home. Seen from a child's perspective they seemed so different so it is very interesting to read about them again as an adult. How we remember things is always affected by who we are, where we were at the time and what was important to us; while large events may have been occurring, it is the 'every day' that consumes us, and that is what we read about in *Snakes Alive*.

The unusual situations that my father faced certainly make interesting reading but, as he records, they have also have made him the person he is. 'Survival of the fittest' indeed applies to him! While he is extremely fortunate to be able to live in such comfortable circumstances during his 'twilight years' in England, I know he remembers with great fondness the tough times that he had to overcome in southern Africa; they will always be the defining years of his life.

Happy reading!

Joy Scott

Preface

It has been a strange journey, especially recalling my youth in England. It has not always been of pleasant memories - making me wish I had done better. I am ashamed of some of it (I must have been a rascal at times) but I have covenanted with myself to 'tell it like it was' so that my family, all born in Africa, have some idea why I am what I am. No apologies; we are a product of our upbringing which, by the Grace of God, has moulded us into who we are today.

I am sorry I did not learn more about my grandparents. In the thirties I remember my paternal grandmother, at Old Marton, being terrified of the telephone! My father did not help; when teaching her how to hold it, he knocked the mouthpiece against her top lip. She nearly fainted. All I know of them is that they lived in Corston, in Bath, and Grandfather was a headmaster. I remember visiting them long before the war and watching them cook a roast of beef on a 'spit'. That was the usual way in many houses those days.

There were five girls and one boy in Mother's family. I knew nothing of her father, but I do remember her mother lying in bed just before she died, in Whittington. That was in the early thirties. So that is one reason why I have written this book – to make sure my family is not as ignorant about the past as I am.

Now that I have written it down, I am amazed at the variety of extraordinary experiences that have occurred in my life:

- semi-blindness
- dangerous encounters with snakes
- attacks from other wild animals, even leading to serious injury
- drink-crazed, violent workers and witch-doctors
- veld fires
- danger of terrorists
- drought and food shortages
- assets wiped out after being the local equivalent of a multimillionaire disastrous drought and subsequent loss of farm

- losing my home and my country after sixty years' service and becoming an economic refugee

Amazingly, I am still alive and kicking, enjoying good health, having a lovely, supportive wife, and am very, very well - still able to tell the tale. God bless my readers and give God the glory!

Happy reading!

Ted Nicholas

Introduction

The first half of this book tells of my life before Africa and the second half of my time in the southern hemisphere. You can choose to read what interests you the most! Much of what I have written is anecdotal, and events recorded are not necessarily sequential. This is simply a book of 'tales' - tales of surviving dangerous encounters in the wild.

Not everybody close to me will necessarily recall the events in an identical way to me, but I have told the stories as I remember them. Laurence is qualified to evaluate my experiences as being genuine because he taught in Zimbabwe and knows their validity. He also fought against the terrorist insurgents.

The thought of recording my memories and experiences for posterity seems to be valid since I am the only one in my family who lived abroad and it would be good for the survivors - my children, nephews, nieces and grandchildren - to know that I was not a 'black sheep' but had a fruitful, exciting and sometimes very painful life outside the UK.

I was not a 'Remittance Man'. (This was someone whose reputation in the country was so bad - a scoundrel, ne'er-do-well - that he had to be sent out to the colonies to preserve the family reputation at home and was then given a monthly 'remittance' to keep him out there! It didn't do the colonies any good; changing his country didn't change his spots.)

If some of my English appears simple – perhaps even immature and repetitive – please understand that I was used to producing notes in English to Africans whose English was their third or fourth language in their repertoire; it had to be kept simple and repetitive. One has to avoid fancy words or expressions. For instance, in the marriage ceremony, the expression "I plight thee my troth" is totally meaningless even to the most sophisticated African! I used to translate it as "I commit myself to keep these promises."

And now follows my story...

Snakes Alive

1

The Beginning

I was born in 1925 in the hamlet of Old Marton near Ellesmere in Shropshire. The hamlet consisted of three farms:

The Hall, Old Marton	(The Lloyds)
Old Marton Hall	(my home)
Old Marton Farm	(The Duttons)

Similarly, the hamlet of New Marton consisted of three farms, one of which belonged to my mother's sister, Aunty Nellie, and her husband, Uncle John Humphries. Their son, Peter, is still alive and is over ninety years old.

I was one of twins, my younger sister (I came out first!) being named Ann. She died in 2009.

We were born into an unusual family; our mother had become married very young (at about eighteen) to a widower next door to her family home at New Marton who had three children: John, Bronnie and Biddy. Mother then had two children, Ian and Pip, their surname being Jenkins. Ian died when he was about five years old and Mother's husband soon followed. (Pip, on the other hand, lived until he was over ninety.) She then married my father and had four children: Jack, Tom, Ann and me. They gave me the name Edward, but I have always answered to 'Ted'.

My father was a good farmer and laboured successfully through the depression of the thirties, despite being responsible for the upbringing of eight children, only four of whom were his own. He hired two permanent labourers: one a wagoner, Billy Vaughan, who dealt with the horses; and the other, Matthew Jones, a general hand but skilled in many farm activities, especially building stacks of hay and corn. During heavy hay and corn harvesting, women from the village would come to help milk the cows by hand since all of us would be carting hay or corn whilst the weather was right, and urgency was necessary.

Mother had a lady who lived in to help her in the house. Her name was, to us, Miss Jones. (Her Christian name was Win but that was too familiar for us to use.)

To gauge the weather forecast my father had a barometer in the sitting room. I was frequently sent from the field to read 'the glass' as it was called since it was housed in a glass cabinet, whether it was rising or falling. Delicate decisions had to be made as to whether or not to continue harvesting late in the evening; if the glass was falling, rain would be imminent. Its progress was recorded on graph paper on a rotating drum which was wound up weekly like a clock. The paper was marked with the time and days of the week and was dated and stored by my father. An arm carrying an ink holder was used for the recording progress. This barometer was part of the furniture all my life at home and operated day and night.

When he married my mother, my father took over the assets in the estate of her late husband, with the proviso that he would pay out the children he inherited, their share of their father's estate. I believe he had to pay out £2000 each when they reached a certain age, and this he did despite the depression - no mean feat in its day! I cannot recall John's face, but I do recall Bronnie and Biddy living at Old Marton, their birthplace.

Dairy farming was the thrust of the farm economy and to keep the cows fed he grew various crops and bred sheep, pigs and poultry to maximise income. He grew oats, kale, mangolds and turnips as cattle feed and grew wheat and potatoes as cash crops. He also made hay for winter feed, making stacks in the field where cattle would be wintered.

It was a skilful job to make a stack of hay to withstand and cope with winter rain and snow. As kids we never thought much about the skill involved in making a haystack; it was just accepted as a natural skill expected of someone you employed. When the stack was completed, a long iron bar with a barb on the end was pushed into the middle of the stack to test its temperature and to draw out a sample of the hay to see if it was being discoloured by heat. Many times the temperature got really hot, but it never resulted in us having to open the stack to stop it catching on fire. It must be remembered that a stack was not always built under perfect conditions; if stacked the slightest bit wet (it could rain whilst being stacked), this caused it to heat up. Stack your lawn clippings and see how quickly the heap gets hot!

Every day a large chunk or wad of hay was cut with a very special, huge knife, and then you carried it on your back and shoulder to the cattle. This, of course, was during the winter. In the worst winter weather of snow, sleet and rain, the rain would freeze on the animals' backs and they would creak as they walked. They would also have icicles hanging from their eyes. It was a gruelling task to carry hay through the snow, but otherwise the animals would have had nothing to eat. Living in such conditions made them hardy stock indeed - and the workers too who had to do the work come rain, snow, sleet or sunshine! It was a tough life; even your trousers could become hardened with ice from the knees down. Cold? I'll say!

Sheep would often be lost under snow drifts as they sheltered under a hedge for protection. The only way to find them was to look for yellow breathing holes coming up through the snow. Sheep also had the infuriating habit of lying on their backs and then being unable to roll back onto their sides so that they could stand up. The evidence of their plight amongst a flock was to see four legs waving in the air. They had to be stood up and held until they regained their balance.

My father was an honourable man. I remember he bought a chicken house at an Agricultural Show and had it delivered to Old Marton, but he never received a bill for it. After about a year he wrote to the sellers advising them of the situation. They wrote back saying they had lost track of the chicken house, thanked him for his honesty, and sold it to him at cost price.

He was a hard man too. I never ever heard him say a kind or affectionate word to my mother - no kiss, no hug, never a touch, smile or word of encouragement over her cooking or housekeeping or any other show of affection. How she stuck it out I don't know. Perhaps in those days nothing else was expected of a husband.

I remember once seeing my mother crying. She was making sandwiches in my junior school days, and I saw a big tear fall on a sultana in a sandwich she was making for me. She said, "Where can we run away to?" It was the most precious sandwich I have ever eaten. I have no idea what their problem was, but I know she had a hard and thankless task with him most of the time. She had to cope with the death of her firstborn son, then her husband and the care of eight children. When work in the field at harvest time was urgent she would have to do the milking too. We accepted this as normal farming life.

I can imagine from his perspective the financial pressures he was facing, being responsible for such a large family during the depression. I don't think he ever liked his stepchildren. Biddy ran away from home to the neighbouring farm, the Duttons, when in her early twenties and never came back. He also resented the costs of Pip's medical needs, visits to doctors and operations.

I can imagine - and *only* imagine - that part of the reason he married my mother was for the immediate financial benefit he obtained by walking into a going concern. That is only speculation but I believe it holds water. However, they stayed together for over fifty years.

He had to be very careful with his money, and there was never much of it around. He refused to give me money to go to the 'flicks' (cinema), saying, "What do you want to go to the pictures for?" I was deeply hurt and can remember the anger in his voice even today. It was done in front of all the family. Knowing the kind of response he might give, it must have been something special for me to have dared to ask him. I cried all the way to the station. Everyone was shocked and there was no further conversation at the breakfast table that morning (or so I was told).

At junior school our pocket money was a halfpenny a week which we were able to exchange at the village shop near Welsh Frankton school for a stick of liquorice and a gobstopper, both costing a farthing each.

For my fifteenth birthday he bought me a scythe! No fancy toys, thank you, but a useful working tool. It was an investment, not a birthday present. He was short of money.

He had some notable sayings:

- "A farmer, when he leaves a farm, must always leave it in a better condition than when he took it over."

- The best manure on a farm was "the farmer's foot".
- "It takes a hundred years to create one inch of soil." (Where he got that from I do not know.)
- Whenever I displeased him, which was quite often, he would finish off with "Whatever next, I wonder!"

I had to dubbin his boots to waterproof them, a job I never enjoyed. We all had to dubbin our boots to keep the water out but I had to do his too.

The apple theft

To get to Welsh Frankton Junior School we had to cross fields, styles and a railway line. There was a lot of mud around, especially around gates where cattle gathered and stirred up the wet soil, and we would arrive at school (and back home again) in a real muddy mess, feet cold and wet.

We had to pass through a farm where the dairy cows stood by a gate before going into the shippon. Always there was a bull amongst them and we were a bit scared of him. It was quite an art to keep some cows between him and ourselves until we reached the gate and escape his notice. His roar when he saw us was frightening and ominous, but we were country children and took this to be the normal way of country life. A really bad-tempered bull would be masked, that is, it would have a metal plate put over its face, like blinkers on a horse, so that it had to raise its head to see underneath. The safety factor was in the fact that a bull always charges with its head down and it couldn't do this with its head up. So whilst it was looking at you underneath its mask it couldn't charge. And as soon as it dropped its head it couldn't see you. Simple!

We also passed a house which had a garden next to the road with a thin hawthorn hedge protecting the garden from intruders walking down the road, including me! There was an apple tree right next to the hedge, and I burrowed a hole underneath it to pinch an apple occasionally. One day when I had successfully stolen an apple and was just about to retreat with my booty, I heard a woman's voice say, "I see you, Ted Nicholas."

That was it! I was found out; I was identified! I would be reported to the police. She knew my name. I was terrified – I was bathed in guilt and sure I was bound for prison. (I was about ten years old at the time. My guilt was enormous!)

We were brought up in a very moral home. I was led to believe - at least it was my perception - that women who wore red were prostitutes, that women certainly didn't smoke or drink or wear trousers, and that they never went to church or to appear before a magistrate without wearing a hat. And if they were divorced... well, what could you expect but someone to infect your family with dreadful morals; so keep them out of your home! We certainly looked down on such people. At least I did! I wonder why it was all to do with women and not men? It seemed that men could do what they liked, but woe betide a woman if she broke the perceived rules of acceptable conduct.

So my guilt rested heavily upon me, and I was certain I had been reported to the police, albeit some six miles away.

The sequel to the story arose a week later when we travelled to Oswestry in our pony and trap which, of course, was open to everyone to see who the occupants were. On the way into town we passed a policeman standing on the side of the road and before we got into town proper. I was certain he was waiting for us; why else would he be standing there right in our way before we even got into the town? If young children could have a heart attack I was a prime candidate. Naturally, I had not told my parents or the rest of the family so they had no idea why I had gone as white as a sheet! Such was the morality of the day. On reflection, we could do with a bit more 'inner guilt' to govern our behaviour today.

This business of women wearing red really came home to me when I was courting Margaret. When walking down a street in Dublin, I think it was, we passed a dress shop where a model was dressed in a gorgeous, billowing, red dress in the window. Margaret asked me what I thought of it. It was a lovely dress and I liked it very much, but to support it was beyond my upbringing. I didn't know what to say because I didn't know her thoughts on red dresses. I hesitated to answer, and she came to my rescue by saying how much she liked it. I was able to agree with her, but she probably thought I was a 'yes man' without a mind of my own. It only goes to show how tenacious teachings to children can be and how they take hold and stick for years. Our brains were computerised even in those days. Gigobytes - Gunge in, gunge out - but at tremendous speed!

The Beginning

School days

On the wall of the school was a wooden board which said "Defense d'affiche" (which I believed was French for "Stick no bills"). What it was doing there goodness only knows since it was a school way out in the country amongst people who couldn't speak French anyway. And who was threatening to put up advertising bills in such a remote, lonely, almost invisible place?

On very wet days Father would take us to school in a pony and trap, the pony being called a 'cob' (a well-understood phrase and description of a certain kind of horse amongst farmers of the day). We had to go the same way to church, which Mother insisted we attended. I always thought it was a bit of a bind since we had to put on Sunday clothes, but I always felt better when I came out. On the way to church I loved to hear the solitary church bell ringing out across the lovely Shropshire countryside "calling the faithful to prayer". It still affects me today when I hear it.

Later on, when I could do more work like milking cows by hand and feeding calves and chickens, I was paid a shilling a month, which was quite a lot but was never quite up to the amount other boys at the Grammar School were given by their parents.

Me with my sister, Ann.

At the junior school I have a few unusual memories.

One day, in about 1936, a helicopter (probably a gyrocopter) flew over the school. I had never seen one before in my life, and Ann came running up to ask me what it was. To this day I think my answer was very clever! I announced with great confidence that it was "a Windmill Aeroplane", no hesitation in my voice at all. Ann accepted it immediately, and I rose up in my own estimation enormously!

My sister was brainier than me at junior school although I didn't

17

recognise it at that time. We had Scripture tests now and then which were verbal. If you did well you were given a certificate. My sister always got one and I never did. I remember one occasion on which this happened. Walking home after school I complained bitterly about Ann getting recognition whilst I was ignored. I complained against the teacher for ignoring me because "I had my hand up many times to answer the question" but was passed by. This was not fair. I too should have had a certificate based on the number of times I had had my hand up. At that time I did not recognise my sister's intellectual superiority even though she always came first in class and I came second.

Another incident stands out. The school abutted a busy main road from Oswestry to Ellesmere. When we played ball games in the playground, quite often the ball went over the wall onto the main road. I went to collect it, obeying the rule when crossing a road to "look right, look left and look right again". This I did, having done it many times before. I was not stupid, knowing the danger. However, I did not see the two cyclists racing down the road. I ran across the road to retrieve the ball and ran into the cyclists but never actually touched them. They were riding just about abreast or nearly so. Although I missed the first one, he braked violently and split his tyre in two. No-one was hurt. I remember the headmaster, Mr Clayton Jones, being unusually solicitous of my welfare, asking me to describe to him in detail what had happened. I cannot recall the outcome with the cyclists.

Another incident at the school terrified me. A boy named Tom died of diphtheria so we all had to have throat swabs taken to see if we were infected. I was the only one who was tested positive, and I lived in fear of death for weeks. Before he died, Tom showed me a green-looking pill he had filched from his mother. He dared me to swallow it, which I did immediately. Much to my horror (and everyone else's) my urine turned green, but I never owned up to what I had done. It cleared up in a day or so.

Another incident had a much more tragic conclusion. It was on a cold winter's day when a teacher, Mrs Jeffries, backed up to the classroom fire to warm herself. A belt of her dress, hanging down the back, caught fire, and I can see her to this day rushing around the classroom trying to beat out the flames. She died. Although it was not in my classroom, I could see her through an open door. It was all over the Daily Mail the next day. As we were assembling to go into school I saw the skin of her hand with her nails attached lying on the ground near the entrance door - a gruesome sight indeed for a young person and has remained in my memory all this time.

One game we played was with 'spinning tops'. These were wooden toys shaped like mushrooms. You started off by spinning the top by hand then striking it with a cord attached to a stick, like a whip, sending it flying through the air and increasing its spinning. The game was to follow it up and do the same again whilst it was spinning, seeing how long we could keep it spinning. It had to be played on a smooth, hard surface - and what better place than the main road? Dangerous stuff!

The village blacksmith made metal hoops for some of us, and these we played with by rolling them along the ground then running after them and keeping them going using a small metal rod - pushing them along and guiding them, turning them this way and that. At least it kept us fit, all that running.

Conkers was a great favourite. You took the seed of a horse chestnut, bored a hole in it, dried it and threaded a string through it with a knot at the end. You then challenged another player to swing his conker against yours and try to break it. You kept a record of how many conkers you had beaten; if your opponent beat you he added your number to his and vice versa. You took it in turns to strike your opponent's conker. Victories were counted in '-ers'. If I had beaten five other conkers mine became a five-er or a fifteen-er or whatever. You had to declare your '-er' status before you started playing.

Yoyos were great fun, and we became quite skilful at making difficult hand changes - over the back of the hand, throwing it outwards and upwards (a difficult one that), sideways and so on. We walked around with a yoyo in our hand doing things subconsciously, like boys practising their bowling action.

Because of the diphtheria scare I had to have my tonsils out at the Oswestry Cottage Hospital when I was twelve, and just before I went to the Grammar School.

I had always had a weakness in this area and can remember waking up in the night having vomited over my pillow. I can still see my mother kneeling beside my bed at two o'clock in the morning, heating olive oil in a teaspoon over a candle, then pouring it into my ear. I don't think it did any good, but it was the remedy at that time.

For the tonsils operation I was laid on the operating table, a cage of cotton wool was put over my face and ether poured over it. When I came round back in the ward I was violently sick, apparently a normal consequence after being anaesthetised with ether. I think I was in hospital for three or four days but I am not sure. I know I went home on a Saturday.

One thing I am sure about is that a farmer was brought in who had broken his leg whilst horse riding when fox-hunting. He moaned dreadfully all night, and I was sure each moan or groan was to be his last. I think he was a Humphries.

Mother

Mother was a very, very fine lady, a saintly woman if ever there was one. She was educated at Howells School in Denbighshire, but I don't know how far she progressed. Before he died, Pip took us there when we were on holiday from Africa, since he had never been there before. He revered our mother because she took him through his difficult childhood, losing his father and having to deal with a stepfather, nursed him, nurtured through sicknesses, operations and the loss of his first son. She was a wonderful foundation for courage and encouragement. When I left for Africa her parting word at Gobowen station was, "Keep your nose to the grindstone and you will not fail." Good advice for today too! Her worst expletive was "drat it" or "bother".

Mother became head of the Women's Institute in Shropshire and once led a delegation of ladies to France on a sightseeing tour. She was then in her late fifties. She taught me the longest word in the world, I believe, which was the name of a Welsh village along with its meaning. It was Llanfairpwllgwyngyllgogerychwyrndrobwyllllantysiliogogogoch!

It means "Saint Mary's church in the hollow of the white hazel near a rapid whirlpool and the church of St.Tysilio of the red cave". I believe at the railway station it is simply 'Llanfair P.G.'!

My mother could also sing the Welsh National Anthem in Welsh. She was not Welsh but there could be some connection in her maiden name, Hayward.

Going back to my father, I never once heard a swear word come out of his mouth, not even the mildest of words. "Dash it" would have been the worst. I had to be educated in the army as to what most of them meant!

He served in the Indian Army at Hyderabad, but I never discovered his regiment nor his duties, what he was doing there and so on. He was a Sergeant Major so must have had some experiences, but I never quizzed him about them nor did he ever volunteer information. Strange, since I spent a lot of time there.

Snakes Alive

The Beginning

Old Marton Hall

My father, circa 1936

The Beginning

Top Left:
Father's sister, Aunty Winnie. Emergency repairs!
Top Right:
The twins
Bottom:
Ted and Margaret at the window of the train at Gobowen on the way to London on my way back to Africa 1953.

Snakes Alive

Top: *Margaret, Mother, Anne Jenkins, Pip's wife.*
Bottom: *Wintery field, Shropshire*

2

Old Marton

Every year we bred ducks, geese and poultry for the Christmas market. We spent days plucking them by hand, and this was a skilful job when done correctly. The art was not to break the skin so that you did not reduce the value of the bird. This was more easily said than done. Geese had 'down' mixed with their feathers, and this had to be plucked separately for pillows. Fingers became very sore after a few days.

During the war a certain friend was involved in the black market. He had a 'kombie' with a false bottom behind the number plate where he had trays to carry his contraband. He would pay high prices for poultry which, during the war, it was illegal for individuals to trade in. I think my father made quite a bit of money out of him.

The story goes (how true I don't know) that a friend from London went to Witney, Pip's first wife's home, and bought a few illegal items such as pheasants, partridges, turkeys, geese, ducks and so on. I know he drove an Alvis car which had a large boot. Just outside London he was stopped at a police road block and asked what he had in the boot. Deciding to come clean, since he could not escape, he rattled off very hurriedly everything he was carrying. The policeman said, "Stop kidding me; don't be so silly!" and sent him on his way. He swore this was true!

Petrol was severely rationed and came in two colours: red for industrial purposes, tractors and engines on the farm; and white for personal use such as shopping and so on. This was very scarce and was controlled by the issuing of coupons. (Food was also controlled by coupons, and when I went on leave from the army I was issued coupons according to the number of days of my leave which I then gave to mother.)

There was more red petrol around so it was easy to fiddle with it. The police would dip your tank and take out a sample. The trick was to make a tube and put it into your tank from the petrol cap, holding maybe half a gallon. Into this you put your white petrol which the police could sample but they could not get into the real tank which would be full of red petrol. The disadvantage and danger of this was that the red petrol would stain your carburettor red; if he lifted your bonnet you would be found out with serious consequences, the worst of which was to be branded a traitor, a Quisling and a friend of the enemy - serious charges indeed.

I went to Oswestry Grammar School in 1937 under the headmastership of Ginger William. I travelled by train every morning, and on the way to school (which was on the other side of the town) I passed a jeweller's shop in the window of which I saw a watch costing seven and six. I coveted this watch with fervour, and it took me eleven months to save enough to buy it. Once I did, I had to let everyone know it by constantly holding it up to my ear every time someone looked at me. Alternatively, I would hold out my left hand with my sleeve well rolled up for everyone to see it! Such pride and yearning for attention!

As we had no electricity we used wet, chargeable batteries for our wireless. This I had to carry to town on the train and drop off with the company which did the re-charging. It cost sixpence a charge, and I spent the day worrying about losing the sixpence.

Sometimes, since I had to carry the battery on my bicycle to the station, I would spill some of the battery acid onto my coat or trousers, eventually burning a brown hole in them. I was not popular although I was never aware of having done it until the hole appeared.

In my very early days, in the early thirties, our milk production was turned into cheese. We had large vats into which the day's milk was poured, anything up to a hundred and fifty gallons or more. The vat had two compartments; the top one held the milk and the one underneath held the hot water to heat the milk.

There were two copper boilers nearby, each shaped like a half-moon with a fire box underneath to hold the coals to heat the water. Once hot enough, the water was carried in buckets by hand and poured into an opening at the end of the vat to take the water underneath the milk. A thermometer was floated in the milk to monitor the temperature, and when this was correct, rennet was added to curdle the milk. When this occurred and the milk was now curds, the moisture (whey) in the vat was drained off and gravity fed it to an underground sump (tank). The curds were then cut up with a five-bladed knife long enough to reach the bottom of the vat. It reminds me of a foot-cleaning grill that one sees in front of a door, but this had a handle at right angles to control it.

This sump was just below my bedroom window and had a perfume of its own. Pig sties were next to the sump so I had pig smells and noises at night as well as the smell from the sump to contend with.

The curds from the vats were transferred to another room where they were converted into cheese, first by draining off excess whey and then by using a press. Cheese cloth was used to line the wooden round container for the curds; then the press was used to squeeze out all the whey. When properly dried or cured, the cheese was removed from its wooden mould and sealed inside the cheese-cloth with a flour and water mixture which, when dry, sealed the cheese. The cheese came out round, weighing more than twenty or thirty pounds. It could be rolled along the ground if you wanted to move it. Our cheese was sold in Ellesmere, and Mother won quite a few prizes for the quality of her product. I believe it was a type of cheddar.

Although I am not certain, I think I remember Mother boring a hole down the centre of the cheese with a specially designed tool, taking out a 'tube' of cheese and filling it with brandy or port or a liqueur and then sealing it off, or plugging the hole, and allowing the liquid to permeate the cheese and give it a distinctive flavour. All sorts of liqueurs might well have been used. Again, they might have been very small cheeses.

Talking about pigs, by law we were allowed to kill one pig a year. I used to hate the actual killing of the pig although I never witnessed the event - it was too gruesome. Hearing it squeal was enough before its throat was cut. When it was dead it was hung up on the back verandah before being dressed. Its hairs had to be removed before the carcase could be cured. This was done by scalding the carcase with boiling water and then scraping the hair off. Then it was quartered and put into a large wooden bath-like container to be cured. Curing consisted of soaking it in salt water, or brine as it was called, and basting it. Every day the parts that were not covered in the wooden bath were bathed or 'basted' in the brine by hand. The bath was never big enough to have the whole carcase covered and completely submerged all at the same time. Once a week or so, all the parts were turned over. This obviously took many days, but when cured adequately the shoulders and hind quarters and the flitch were hung up in the kitchen to carry on with the maturing and curing process. They were covered in cheese cloth to protect them from flies and to absorb any liquid oozing from the carcase.

The middle part - that is the part between the front and hind quarters - was called the 'flitch', and it was from this our bacon came. It was hung up by two hooks which were attached to larger hooks embedded in the black oak beams in the ceiling of the kitchen. It was an old house, probably over three hundred years old, and most houses of that era had large oak beams as part of the kitchen construction.

There were many side products of a pig killing. We made our own sausages and other by-products such as brawn, but my favourite by far were the 'Savoury Ducks'. They consisted of all the scraps of meat prunings or trimmings from the various products, mixed together (no matter where they came from) and rolled into a ball about the size of a meatball. Mother would then lay out on a table the 'net' (fatty muscle or diaphragm) that lay between the heart, lungs and the stomach. This was laced in appearance. She would take a lump of the meat, cut a piece of the diaphragm to fit, wrap it around the meat, then fry it. Talk about heavenly food! You couldn't beat it!

When I came home on leave from the army, no matter what time of the day, Mother would take down a flitch and cut a slice of bacon about two feet long, cut it into three pieces and fry it with the Savoury Ducks, if there were any, plus homemade sausages, fried bread, eggs and tomatoes, sheep's liver and any other available delicacies. Put this lot into a large (and I *mean* large) frying pan on an Aga stove and you had a soldier ready to desert the army! I often wonder if I ever thanked her enough for her understanding love.

Husbands, take note. Encourage your wives and thank them daily for their diligence in feeding you three times a day, every day. If you don't, you may regret it when they are no longer with you. And children, never fail to acknowledge the daily commitment of your mother feeding you three times a day to keep you healthy. I certainly regret not being certain of what I said to my mother.

The two copper boilers also provided bath water for the Saturday night bath. The boiling water had to be carried in large five-gallon buckets along the outside shed, through the kitchen, then the dining room and then into the bathroom. It was an acquired skill to have the right amount of hot water to keep the bath water at the acceptable temperature for successive children and to have enough for your parents so that they did not have to go out in the frosty air to fill the bath up again. Having a bath was hard work but could not be avoided.

In later times it became more profitable to sell whole milk, and cheese production ceased. I shall always remember the taste of the curds before being processed into cheese - far nicer than the finished product.

We had oodles of cream in the house! The evening milking was stored in ten-gallon churns. By morning the cream would have risen to the top, and it was simple to take a jug and dip it into the cream. We had cream on our porridge, cornflakes, puddings and always in our tea. To me, only poor people had milk in their tea!

Income was also derived from egg production from poultry on free range. They slept in wooden chicken houses holding perhaps a hundred hens, probably less, with nest boxes for them to lay their eggs. They had to be fed twice a day with chicken mash in troughs and grain scattered on the grass, morning and evening. This they had to scratch for if the grass was long. It was natural for them to do so.

Poultry were subject to infection by minute lice, and their perches and nest boxes had to be creosoted frequently. At night they had to be locked up against foxes, using a 'pophole' for exit and entry which had to be closed at night and opened in the morning. One night when performing this duty, I went to one poultry house and closed the pophole. My half-brother Pip saw me and asked what I had done. I told him I had dropped the pophole door into place. "That is strange!" he said because he had just done the same thing. I went back and found I had opened it! Horrors! What would have happened if a fox had got in? I know I would have been severely punished for sure, and I would have deserved it. "Whatever next!" my father would have said.

We had about half a dozen such houses scattered around the farm, and it was a serious business (and quite a long one) if you were doing it on your own. In the summer this was a problem because for one thing you had to wait until it was getting dark and on a bright summer's evening it could be quite late before the hens would go inside. One thing you could not do was to be impatient. You could not drive hens into their house; they would go every which way when driven. Sometimes it could be 10.30pm or so before you got to bed and this after a busy day's work on the farm with another early start the next day.

I remember going to shut up a pen of cockerels we were fattening, only to find that I had not let them out in the morning. I let them out and most of them rushed off for water, but some started eating dock leaves. I never told anyone about this for fear of getting into trouble, but I made sure I let them out early the next day and gave them an extra ration of food to make up for the loss they suffered the previous day. I can still feel the guilt as I think about it!

One of the most hateful jobs I ever had was to wash the hen's eggs for sale. They could be covered in droppings which, when dry, were difficult to remove. The eggs were sold in cases every week, each case holding perhaps twenty dozen eggs. I often had to clean eggs whilst the rest of the family played cricket or soccer - a great snivelling time for me on many occasions, I can assure you! I used to cheat by putting dirty eggs at the bottom of the box instead of washing them. I was never found out!

We hatched our own chicks through two incubators, each holding a hundred eggs. The heat was provided by paraffin burners which had constantly to be serviced to keep an even temperature. All the eggs had to be marked at one end because they had to be turned every day and one needed to know which end was which and also to turn them evenly.

We had to buy in chicks which had been 'sex linked' as the term was, so that we could be sure we were buying pullets and not a mixture of pullets and cockerels, which was the case with our own hatchings. We bought them in boxes of a hundred, but the seller always put three extra chicks in, in case of death. Just think... these days my nephew Robin deals in thousands of day-old chicks at a time; how times change!

There were many breeds of chickens to choose from, our favourite being Rhode Island Reds and then White Wyandottes. The former produced brown eggs, the latter white. For ducks we bred Aylesburys and not Muscovies. These which were larger but undisciplined; they would fly all over the place, landing and sleeping on tops of buildings and houses, leaving an awful mess behind. The 'Runner duck' was another breed with high mobility but was smaller and less meaty (not a quality that a large family appreciated!) I cannot remember having turkeys at Christmas time although I do remember feeding the turkey chicks chopped onion tops.

Another painful memory is of the day I nearly blinded the village blacksmith, Joe. He was a very fine blacksmith indeed, of the old school. If you go to Col. Kenyon's Estate, Hardwick Hall, near Ellesmere, you will see the most impressive entrance gates to the estate, made by him entirely of wrought iron without the aid of electric or acetylene welding.

Every so often I would have to take a horse to be shod. We had large Shire cart horses, and I would ride them to the Smithy. They were big beasts, but I was never afraid to ride one; we were all familiar with them, and they with us, because we worked with them constantly. It was never a comfortable ride. Their backs were so broad that you nearly had to do the splits to stay on! Sometimes I would walk the horse because if I got off it to open a gate I could not get back on again; it was too tall.

On this particular day I had taken a horse to be shod. Whilst waiting for something, Joe had heated a piece of flat iron red hot and asked me to help cut it in half. To do this he held a very strong chisel, designed for this purpose, at the point to be cut. The chisel was held by Joe with a long metal handle so that he would not be burned whilst holding it. That is why he needed help - another hand or arm, as it were. He held the iron with a pair of long-handled pliers in his left hand and the chisel in his right.

He gave me a heavy, long-handled two handed hammer - one that you had to raise over your head to give power to your blow. It was probably a fifteen pound hammer which I was not unfamiliar with. I raised it high above my head and gave the chisel all I had got!

Unfortunately, in trying to show off my skill in such a situation, my aim on the chisel head was a bit off centre. The hammer head slipped off the head of the chisel sideways and, unseen by Joe or me, it hit a small piece of metal lying on the anvil. It flew up and opened Joe's cheek a fraction below his eye. An inch higher and he would have lost his eye.

To make matters worse, and much to my chagrin, other people were watching, including some cousins from Weston-super-Mare. They were 'townies', and my incompetence with the hammer hurt all the more. Such is pride!

It was fascinating to see how Joe shaped a shoe for each hoof and then, after heating it to his satisfaction, would lift the horse's hoof onto his leg and bend the shoe onto the hoof to make a perfect fit. The hot shoe would sizzle into the hoof which, I suppose, could be compared to a human toe-nail. With specially shaped nails the shoe was fixed to the hoof to secure it in place. The smell of the burning 'nail' (or hoof) of the horse and the smoke of it enveloping Joe's face are abiding memories.

Shire horses, due to their size and the heavy work they did in every sort of soil type, including very wet ones, were shod with heavy shoes. Race horses on the other hand were shod with 'racing plates', half the weight or even less than the working Shires.

In the thirties, all our heavy work was done by horses - ploughing, carting manure, hay and corn. We did not have a tractor or motor car until the forties.

Ploughing with horses was a great art. It was wonderful to watch our wagoner, Billy Vaughan, ploughing a ten acre field with two horses and a single furrow plough. It cut a furrow a foot wide so you can imagine the distance he covered walking in a day, guiding and controlling the plough and horses hour after hour.

It was also an amazing sight to see seagulls following the plough, crying their cry and eating the worms which were exposed when the sod was turned. We must have lived some fifty miles from the sea so how they knew where to come at just the right time goodness only knows. And they would be there the next day so where they slept was also a mystery.

Joe was an expert at putting iron rims on wooden wagon wheels, making them perfectly round and shaped exactly (and I mean exactly) to fit tightly. He would then heat the rim to expand it, put it over the wooden wagon wheel and pour water over it to contract it tightly on the wheel. These wagons carried heavy loads of hay and corn so his work was always being tested. I never saw a rim fall off and we had many such wagons, as did all the other farmers around the village.

Joe's son, Alf, was my best friend in junior school in Welsh Frankton - a village between Ellesmere and Whittington in Shropshire. Later, Alf decided to write a history of his village life in a book and, hopefully, donate the proceeds to the hospital in which he had recovered after a heart attack. He called the book 'Me Dad's the Village Blacksmith'.

It was a great success so he wrote a sequel 'Following me Dad' and a third, the title of which I cannot remember. Because of Alf's reputation from the sale of his books and after-dinner speeches, his 'Smithy' became a tourist attraction. Tourists came by bus to watch Alf's older brother Jack make a horse shoe from scratch, and then it was raffled to raise money. I was once there when a bus load of tourists arrived, and from the laughter coming out of the smithy I could tell that Jack had made their journey worthwhile.

One other memory comes to mind. Joe had two sons. When his wife became pregnant again, she eagerly desired a daughter. Tradition or superstition had it that if she would walk backwards up the stairs to bed she would have a daughter. It didn't work and out popped a son - Alf!

Another form of income was from wild rabbits. We had plenty of them in various parts of the farm. I remember one amusing incident when Tom came home saying he had seen a rabbit burrow 'sniving' with black rabbits, a fairly unusual phenomenon. 'Sniving' implied 'a large number', 'floods of' or 'lots of' whatever was being described. When asked to elucidate he said there were at least four!

A railway line marked the edge of one end of the farm and this was a great source of supply because it was cut into a bank to level the gradient a bit. This gave the rabbits a good place to burrow because they did not have to burrow down but straight in. 'Rabbiting' (or more correctly 'ferreting') on the railway line was illegal so when we heard a train coming we had to hide among grass and bushes. If we were seen, the train driver would shout at us, but we never heard anything more.

We used ferrets to catch the rabbits in their burrows. We tied a strong line with a collar around the ferret's neck and sent it down the rabbit hole. In this environment rabbits always had 'bolt holes' which were well disguised by grass and shrubs. The art was to find them first and cover them with nets because as soon as you put a ferret in the burrow a rabbit would bolt out in fear, thus being entrapped by the net.

When all was quiet and the ferret did not return we would dig down and follow the line, often finding the ferret had gathered a number of rabbits at the end of the hole. Often you could hear the ferret scratching the rabbit's back trying to remove its hair so that it could get to its flesh. You could find four or more rabbits at the end of the hole.

Ferrets had very sharp teeth, and one had to be very careful when handling them to avoid being bitten. At school we bragged about how many ferrets we had, this to show our 'townie' friends how lacking in experience they were of country life and, therefore, how superior we were to them. Kids!

I think that father used to sell a pair of rabbits for seven shillings and six pence.

3

School

I did not do too well at school, my twin sister outshining me all the time. She was very clever academically. A year before I did, she took nine subjects at Cambridge and got nine distinctions. A year later I took only five subjects and got five credits. I never really liked her after that; she was too brainy! I only ever had one thing over her which she could not deny: I was her older brother!

Because of lack of money I had to wear patched trousers to school which offended me greatly. So even in the hottest, dry summer days I would wear a raincoat to cover the patches. Mother tried to persuade me to tell my father why I wore a raincoat on dry summer days, but I was too scared to say anything. I was always afraid of him when I was a boy at home.

A big disadvantage we had as a boys' school was that when war broke out our younger masters (they were not called teachers) were conscripted into one of the forces and, horror upon horrors, they were replaced by 'skirts'! A woman had never been seen on the school grounds before, and now we, the elite, had to suffer this indignity (or so we reasoned then).

The war tore apart our education. Many of our young masters were called up. Our science master, a Mr Oddy, was killed within two months of joining up and was never replaced, which limited my choice of a career. My father wanted me to be a vet, but I never had the schooling to qualify me for entry into university.

Snakes Alive

Certainly the war had a big influence on boys of the time. We were more interested in learning how to kill Germans, and to this end, as a sixteen year old, I joined the Air Training Corp (ATC). I had a blue uniform and attended lessons on how to navigate an aeroplane, how to calculate the effect of winds, head winds and cross winds on our ETA (Estimated Time of Arrival). We were full of such language at school! We had aircraft identification classes and tests so that we, in our dreams, did not shoot down the wrong aircraft. We learned the difference between magnetic north and true north and the difference between longitude and latitude, time zones etc. We enjoyed it immensely but in my case all to no avail because I joined the army!

Oswestry Grammar school was the second oldest school in England, the oldest being Winchester Grammar School. The school playing fields, the 'Maesyllan', was the scene of a battle between a pagan and a Christian king in about 1000 AD, the pagan king winning. By the way, Oswestry gets its name from King Oswald. He held court under a tree which, naturally, was known as 'Oswald's Tree'. So the story goes... it sounds good anyway.

My school was founded in 1407 and the original buildings are still there. I took my children to see them a few years ago, and on the lych gate into the Anglican Church grounds is carved the year 1407. That church is reputed to have the widest church aisle in the country and also has a placard listing the name of every minister since the church was built around 900 AD.

Probably our most famous pupil was A.W. Spooner 1844-1930. He transposed consonants with amusing results, like saying "hush my brat" instead of "brush my hat" and "Kinkering congs their titles take" instead of "Conquering kings..." etc. It came to be known as Spoonerism. He became a clergyman and was famous for his deft use of words.

Both my brothers went to the same school before me but I have little recollection of them being there, especially Jack.

On the wall of the school exit road, a wall of a neighbouring property but high enough to exclude any view of it, are plastered the words 'Last Day'. In 1850, on his last day at school, a boy took a piece of chalk and scribbled 'Last Day' on the wall, since he was leaving school that day for good. It really *was* his last day; as he ran out of the school gate he was killed by a passing horse and carriage. His words have been kept in whitewash ever since.

I remember Tom being struck in the face by a football, heavy with mud. In those days footballs were made of leather and were very heavy when wet with mud. The ball was booted by a master so it carried weight and speed. It flattened him and poor Tom's face was bright red for hours.

My school career was uneventful. I played first team soccer and cricket and was a 'fives' champion. Fives was squash played with a gloved hand instead of a racquet.

I recall one amusing incident which embarrassed me no end. Because I lived so far away from school, some six miles, I had a hot lunch provided by the school and in their dining room. It was a boarding school so it had such facilities. There were very large tables provided, some being over two hundred years old. Some boys had carved their names and dates on them. The table I sat at (we always sat in the same place) held twelve pupils. I sat at one end, and a lad named Frank Barratt sat at the other.

Frank was at the lower end of the ladder academically, as it were, Maths being one of his worst subjects. If he got ten out of a hundred in a Maths test he was delighted because he had reached double figures! One lunchtime he called out to me in a loud voice, "Ted, have you heard of the new way of counting sheep?"

Before continuing with this story I should mention that I was very jealous of Frank in one respect. At fifteen years old he was a sheep dealer. This was in about 1940. Frank would spend weekends dealing in sheep instead of doing homework. He was well known for his local knowledge and expertise and farmers would phone him and ask him where they could buy a tup (a male sheep or a ram) or where they could sell some ewes and so on. Frank probably didn't know what a ram was - a tup was a tup, stupid!

Frank always made money on these deals and made more money in a weekend than I earned in a year. And now he was asking me about a new way of counting sheep.

I knew how to count sheep; you ran them against a fence, put a stick in front of the first sheep and she would jump over it. The next sheep would do the same, and if you took the stick away the following sheep would jump over the imaginary stick. It was easy to count them one at a time. Now this country yokel, who wore yellow socks at weekends (or so I am told) was challenging me publicly to tell of a better way. I was a numbers man, who could get 90% in a Maths test, but now being forced publicly to display my knowledge - or lack of it. I went through all my experience in about thirty seconds flat, but was absolutely flummoxed. I didn't know the answer nor what to say in front of everyone listening - maybe twenty or more boys. There were probably no more than seventy pupils in the whole school at that time i.e. during the war.

This yokel was holding me up to ridicule. I raced through all my knowledge of counting aids but had no answer. Frank obviously had come across some modern technique in his sheep dealings which was new to me. These thoughts raced through my mind for about thirty seconds but I had to give up. I just couldn't imagine "a new way of counting sheep" as Frank put it.

He said, "Ya, it is easy; just count their legs and divide by four!" Ever been had? Ever felt like a fool? I had to admit defeat in this case and Frank won a notable victory; his reputation was much enhanced at my expense.

Pip was unable to join the armed forces because of his physical disability. Instead, he went farming near Sandbach in Cheshire and was very successful.

At the beginning of the war, Jack left home to join the Air Force. He trained as a pilot despite a deformed right hand. As a youngster, he put his hand into the mouth of a kibbling machine, which grinds oats into cattle feed, and lost two fingers - his little finger and the one next to it on his right hand. Despite this he won his wings and was sent to Canada as a Flying Instructor. He married Joan whom he met in the Air Force and had seven children. Strangely enough, soon after their engagement I had lunch with her brother in Mumbai (then called Bombay), India.

Brother Tom was not allowed to serve in the armed forces because his occupation (food production) was deemed too important for the nation. He and countless other farmers' sons like him have never had their services recognised by the nation. This is a tragedy for even Land Army girls have had such recognition. His work was so onerous in summer he would lose a stone in weight every year.

He married Ted Lloyd's daughter, Margaret, and farmed close by. He had a pedigree flock of sheep – Suffolks – and even exported them to Russia, along with his father-in-law's sheep. His knowledge was such that he became a well-known judge of his breed of sheep and was invited to officiate at the Royal Agricultural Show – an honour indeed to be so invited to officiate at the finest Agricultural Show in the world. Probably his highest honour in this area was to be invited to teach Diana, Princess of Wales, the finer points in sheep breeding and judging. Tom also became a magistrate in Oswestry, another feather in his cap. Well done, Tom! He is now eighty eight.

Talking of feathers, during the war when he was forced to work on the land, someone sent him a white feather in the post - an insult indeed because a white feather signified cowardice.

He built up a beautiful flock of pedigree Suffolk sheep but most unfortunately, like many others at the time, lost his life's work through a foot and mouth epidemic.

Schooldays

There were three schools in Oswestry: The Girls' High School, The Boys' High school and the Grammar School. At one time, very many years ago, this last was known as:

> The School,
> Oswestry.

Hence our sense of superiority!

School started at 9 am but was preceded by a service, daily in the school chapel – a fine little building with its own organ. We who lived on the Ellesmere side of the town never got to this service because we lived too far away and, having to come by train, could never get to school in time because of the railway timetable.

At Old Marton our day started early with farm chores, breakfast at eight, then a bicycle ride to the railway station a mile and a half away to catch a train at around 8.30am.

Our bicycles were kept in a 'loose box' (a small shed used to house calves or sheep - animals which were not tied up but kept loose.) It was always a problematic moment every morning when going into the shed in case your bicycle had a flat tyre. Then it was too late to repair it, and it meant a mad rush to run, run, run to the station to catch the train! A short cut had to be taken through someone's field, then through a barbed wire fence onto the platform. If you missed this train you had to wait two hours for the next one. I never missed it but had many a close shave. Trains were always on time so there was no such thing as hoping it would be late for your sake.

The railway line was a 'branch line' meaning it was of secondary importance in the railway network. This line was part of the Great Western Railway (GWR) and operated in the west of the country from London Paddington station up to Glasgow.

This branch line attracted the smaller steam engines and carriages while the 'Flying Scotsman' (a huge engine capable of over a hundred miles per hour) was reserved for the main lines. The steam engines which pulled our carriages varied in size but were all small since the journeys were short and did not have very heavy goods to pull. Speeds rarely exceeded thirty miles per hour. Gradients were generally even so no great power was needed.

Our morning train carried businessmen and women who were going to work in Oswestry, coming from as far afield as some twenty five miles away and arriving in Oswestry for nine o'clock opening. It was also a favourite for school children going to the three main schools. Boys and girls never mixed on the train, mainly because we were too shy and gauche. Most of us were unsophisticated country kids and, as boys, were terrified of girls, not knowing how to talk to them in such close surroundings. At least, that was my response!

The carriages seated about eight or ten passengers in each compartment, four or five facing each other about three feet apart with a rack for satchels and brief cases etc. above each set of seats. Underneath the seats was a radiator through which steam was passed to heat the carriage in winter. Over the entrance side of the compartment was a chain running through a small pipe the length of the carriages. This was an emergency stop device. If you pulled the chain down it activated emergency brakes and the train came to a screaming, shuddering halt. An inspector would then come and look into each compartment to find out what the trouble was. I only remember it happening once when a boy took down his satchel from the rack and it caught the chain accidentally. It was heavy with books, and there was nothing he could do when it got entangled with the chain.

As boys we played a nasty trick on the girls by making 'stink bombs' and throwing them into the compartments occupied by girls. The trick was to take some film negatives, especially rolls of cine films, roll them tightly in a ball, wrap them in newspaper like a Christmas cracker, then light one end of it. When the flame reached the roll of film it billowed out with smoke of the foulest smell. We always thought this was funny!

I met my first girlfriend on this train. How we started is a bit of a mystery. She was part of Ann's class at the Girls' High and we somehow looked at each other and were pleased by what we saw. When leaving Welsh Frankton Station she was going on to Ellesmere and was leaning out of the carriage window so I waved to her and she waved enthusiastically back. From then on we used to meet on the train each morning and secretly held hands and passed soppy love notes to each other. We were aged about fifteen.

We were so secretive that Ann knew nothing about it. The girl's name was Rhoda Atkinson and she used to cycle four miles to meet me secretly on a lane near Old Marton most Sunday afternoons. I could never leave the farm to go to see her because of farm work so she came to see me when others in the house were having a Sunday afternoon nap. I think she must have had a crush on me; what a boost to my ego! What her parents thought of their daughter disappearing for an hour or so every Sunday afternoon I never discovered.

Many of us were dedicated to autograph albums. As boys we only asked girls to sign them. This was a way of measuring our popularity with the opposite sex. My own girlfriend was an artist, or so it seemed because she drew a lady dressed in an expensive fur coat. I wondered it was a hint... Another girl wrote, "Speech is silver, silence is gold." I took the hint and never spoke to her again!

Back to the trains. There were no mechanical signalling systems once the train left a main station like Oswestry. It travelled to the next main station purely on an agreed timetable. A 'ganger' controlled and serviced physically all the railway line and any station siding. He operated the points by hand. When there was thick fog he would put two detonators on the rails, about ten yards apart; when a train ran over them and they went *bang, bang* the train driver knew he was near a station and would close his engine down and coast into the unseen station. It worked very well.

Each steam engine had a sand box above and in front of the leading driving wheel. When there was snow or ice on the rails he would mechanically open the box and trickle fine sand on the rails so that the driving wheels could get a grip and not just spin around on the ice.

On the engine was a driver and a stoker whose job was to shovel coal into the firebox to keep up steam pressure. It was a most gruelling task. Each engine carried its own coal and water.

Each train had a guard who was responsible for setting the train off on its next journey. He had to make sure all the doors were shut – nothing automatic of course – then blow a strong blast on his whistle and turn the lamp he was carrying to green; wave it to the driver, who responded with a whistle; and off we would go. All very simple.

The railway line was one boundary of the farm, and we could see the trains. In winter at night a passenger train, fully lit up, would go by and mother would explain, "It was the devil running away with a row of houses."

Oswestry was an intermediate station for people travelling from mid-Wales to the north. They had to change trains, and the station foreman would call out, "All change, all change for those going to Gobowen, Ruabon, Wrexham and the north via Crewe." Many of the passengers were from Liverpool and Lancashire and had their particular accents. I remember one of my friends saying, when he heard such an accent, "I bet he eats his peas off a knife!" It seemed a strange talent to me, but he assured me it was true. It only goes to show we have many hidden gifts!

As I said, school lessons started at 9am, and we had to rush to get there in time as the school was the other side of town, about a mile away. This we were not too keen to do, but the headmaster didn't let us off the hook and would suddenly appear at the entrance gate and on to the main road to see if we were running. Most of the time we were not, but when we saw him we would break out into a gallop which only proved our guilt and did not fool the headmaster, a strict disciplinarian.

There were about twenty-five to thirty boarders, some coming from as far away as South Africa. There was also a Junior School on the premises. We each had our own desk with hinged lids. Each one had a hole in the top-right-hand side to hold an ink pot. We had no fountain pens but wrote with pens that had replaceable nibs attached to a handle (like that of a pencil) which we then dipped into the ink pot. Much blotting paper was needed. Fountain pens were too expensive. We also used pencils extensively. (Even when I joined the army I wrote my first letter home in pencil.) Classes were very small – maybe 15 at the most.

All our masters were either Oxford or Cambridge graduates but, unlike other schools, they never wore gowns. It never bothered us but now I wonder why. They wore suits or sports jackets. Most of them boarded at the school. One of them, a Mr. D. G. W. Felton, had played cricket for Oxford University earlier in the century but was now somewhat corpulent. Since he was our French master his nickname was 'Fatty Foiton'. He taught us that you could really speak French well if you could understand an excitable Frenchman speaking on a transatlantic telephone. He also taught us scripture, and to this day I can see him demonstrating instant obedience through the story of Abraham and Isaac. Just as Abraham was about to plunge his knife into Isaac, a voice called from heaven. Mr. Felton told us that Abraham didn't say, "Wait a minute! I am busy and will answer you when I have finished this job. Give me a bit of time and I will do what you want." I can see him standing beside a radiator demonstrating his story with waving arms.

One boy got away with an outrageous story when we were given a boring subject for a homework essay. He didn't like the essay subject so changed it to an outlandish cowboy story which involved one cowboy shooting the other. He made so many holes in the other cowboy that when the wind blew it played 'Auld Lang Syne'.

Every week we had singing lessons in the chapel. I hated that, fearing that I would be asked to sing a solo to see what kind of voice I had. It never happened so I was never relieved of the tension. One boy, Peter Birch, had the most lovely alto voice, and his rendition of the 'Nunc Dimittus' was extraordinarily beautiful. Our teacher, Dr. Nicholas, was a professional organist and was invited to play a thirty minute organ music recital on the BBC.

Another master, Mr. James, played football for Cambridge University. It was he who kicked a wet, leather, mud-laden football into Tom's face, instantly flattening him.

Lessons were of forty five minute duration with a fifteen minute break in between. My writing was apparently poor, and I was not allowed to go to the playground but had to stay in and practise better writing from an example book. Lessons finished at 4.30 and our train home left at 5.30. We mooched around town looking for girls to chat up, but we were very shy about it. We met outside Woolworths which had a department called 'Nix over Six' meaning that no item in this department cost more than sixpence. Not much of a draw to me because I never had such money!

The dining room in the school was a large room holding probably sixty children, mostly boarders. The masters sat at one table at the top of the room whilst the boys sat at others at right angles to the head table. The food was pretty awful, especially the cabbage, which was always swimming in water (why, I don't know!)

Wednesday and Saturday afternoons were sports practice afternoons. It was always embarrassing for us as we had to ask permission to leave in order to catch the train home. Once a year we had a sports day with all the usual events. We competed by 'houses' and competition was fierce! We had only one local school to compete with in other sports such as football and cricket (being wartime, which meant we could not travel and no-one could come to us). That was the Boys' High School. I played in the first team of both disciplines. I also played 'fives' successfully. It was squash played with a gloved hand instead of a racquet

Once a year we held a school concert and play, but since play practices were held in the evenings I could not take part. The only contribution I could make was to sell chocolates and sweets during the interval. I had a large tray of goodies which I carried with a belt around my neck and with two handles at the side. I walked up and down the two aisles selling chocolates, sweets, chewing gum and whatever. When the play was due to start or when I had satisfied the market I went to the back and sat down on a chair. That was my plan, but another boy had different ideas. Just as I sat down, and at the crucial moment, he pulled the chair away. There was an awful crash with money and goods scattered all over the floor and angry looks coming from the audience. Never again!

We had swimming once a week, but I never learned to swim at school. Where I did, I can't remember. I used to be so envious of those who could jump off the diving board and do such marvellous things. The lessons were held in the town swimming pool.

Every year we had a special prize-giving day for school achievements. There were always guests and dignitaries invited. Much to our disgust we had to wear Eton collars on that day. These were large, white, heavily starched collars, and we were teased by other boys and girls on the train when we appeared in such outlandish dress.

We had a school uniform of grey trousers and shorts, a grey jersey and navy jacket with the school badge on the pocket. We wore navy caps with the school badge on the front. This was a silver shield with an inverted V across it. We wore white shirts with van Heusen detachable collars and a school tie. Even though we changed our school clothes for farming clothes when we got home it was inevitable that we smelled somewhat like a farmyard!

During the war, school life became much orientated around military matters and as a school we did well in earning military awards. I was awarded the 'belt' at Sandhurst, the second highest honour the Royal Military College could award to a cadet, and a boy whose surname was Charles and who was a bit of a 'wet' at school was awarded the highest honour at the Royal Airforce training centre at Cranwell. That's where he showed his true talent. No other school in the area gained such honours.

There was one boy who always achieved the highest marks in all his subjects and left us all behind annoyed us and made us very jealous although we would not admit it. We excused our lack of competing with him by saying he was different from us because he was a 'swot' – a most terrible and heinous crime in our view! Quite unreasonably we put our failures down to him 'swotting' at night whilst we were playing soldiers. Swots were at the lower end of the popularity scale or at least the 'to be admired' scale. Unreasonably we blamed him for our poor exam results. How could we be successful when we had a swot in our midst, setting impossible standards for us to follow and whilst we were learning to fight the enemy? He upset the whole rhythm of the war-torn school who were more interested in killing Germans than getting good exam results. He showed us all up and we didn't like it or him. He was like a sore thumb... but we were never too proud to ask his advice on tricky maths or science problems! What an issue we made out of nothing! He later became a doctor.

"Manners maketh man" we were taught. When I was on leave from the army and dressed in my military uniform, I visited the school one Saturday afternoon and sat next to the headmaster watching a cricket match. Close to the end of the game, a boy who was compelled to watch, had to leave to go home. This was not unusual, but when he walked past the headmaster he gave the head a perfunctory flick of his fingers and a tug at his forelock in acknowledgement. I was indignant and said to the head, "Surely that boy should have raised his cap to you - and if not to you, at least to me as a visitor." The head took it seriously and said he would address the school on Monday. Such was our upbringing! Respect for authority! The army taught you that, and so did our parents. My father once saw me talking to my mother with my hat on. I had a mouthful on that day and deserved it.

A thought about my father comes to mind. He was a patriotic man, and during the war a group called 'Local Defence Volunteers (LDV)' was formed (also known as the Home Guard) in which he was appointed a sergeant – a rank he had held in the army during the First World War. Every night some of them met in an empty chicken house on Peter Humphries' farm to listen for aircraft flying overhead. They had to record the time and perceived direction the aircraft was flying in. Where the information went I do not know! It was an all night duty, and all local farmers and workers were involved. All of them had to go to work the next day; no excuses! This happened in all the towns and villages with men working nights under the 'Air Raid Precautions (ARP)' system. They would report bombings and fires to the relevant authorities. They worked from rooftops for best viewing.

School

Top: *Oswestry School in the 1960s*
Bottom: *'Last Day' chalked on the wall in 1850 and renewed ever since*

Oswestry School Chapel

4

Home

Home life was a bit under stress. Biddy left home and became a house-keeper for a well-to-do farmer. They lived about fifteen miles away and their farm was bombed by the Germans. Apparently, one German pilot dropped his bombs some time before reaching Liverpool – the farm being on their flight path to that city – probably to avoid the intense flak surrounding the city. Sometimes, when there were no clouds, we could see it from Old Marton, but we could not hear it. Incendiaries were dropped as well. One struck the eaves of the house and lodged in the woodwork at the side of the roof. It burned readily enough but did not set the house on fire, which was a miracle. Fires were started in the stackyard, and German bombers targeted them. They had to let out the dairy cows, which were in the shippon, being winter. Their horses were terrified but had nowhere else to go except into the open field. After a day or so we went to see the farm and found many fields in the area pitted with bomb craters.

One day we had our own excitement and contact with the air war. We noticed a small aeroplane circling our farm and others around and about. It was a Miles Magister training aircraft no higher than two hundred feet and so with minimum visibility for the pilot. After a considerable time of flying around, trying to identify the roads and villages in order to ascertain his location, he landed in one of our fields. We rushed down to claim him before any neighbours could; after all, he had landed in *our* field and therefore it was up to us to help him!

He was about nineteen years old and was on a navigational training flight. He had got lost when the weather had closed in, and he had not been able to find his way back to base. We were thrilled to have a *real* pilot in our home and spent much time in admiring his training stories.

He telephoned his base, some fifty miles away, and a flying instructor motored to the farm the next day. He had to bring fuel with him because the trainee pilot had consumed most of his supply when flying round and round, and there was not enough left to get him back to base. The instructor flew the aircraft out, the pilot returning in the air force vehicle which brought the instructor to us. Such excitement for us!

Biddy never married but her elder sister, Bronnie, did. She married a well-to-do farmer, Eddie Holbrooke, and had three boys. The eldest one was running the farm, but he died when a tractor he was driving turned over on top of him, burning him to death as he was pinned underneath.

Part of their farm was low-lying and bordered the river Dee. There we learned to put out night lines to catch fish, especially a variety called 'flat fish', which were delicious to eat. In late winter the river flooded from melting snows in the Welsh mountains; the silt covered the low fields and fertilised them for free. When the floods eventually subsided (sometimes after weeks) and rain fell to wash the silt off the grass, it was as if a lot of fertiliser had been applied. For the farmer it was excellent early spring grazing after the cows had been fed hay in the dairy for months. It was a welcome change of diet and immediately boosted milk production and income.

Some holidays we would go and stay with them for a week or so. We would be picked up in their car for the fifteen mile journey. I was a poor traveller so the car had to be stopped in order that I could vomit on the side of the road. I never endeared myself to this family because of this, and I dreaded going there and coming back. I was led to believe I was the 'sickly one' in the family (which in these circumstances I think I really was).

Eddie loved horse racing and would bet on the races. With the limited understanding of a child, I considered him to be very knowledgeable. For the holiday I was given twelve pennies - a fortune to me! With Eddie's great knowledge I knew I had a chance to increase my capital. So, taking his advice, I would bet a penny with him on the horse he said was bound to win. "Can't be beaten!" he would say. Those horses never did win, however, and my capital was reduced to half. Back at their home I looked so miserable he gave me back my pennies!

Their neighbour's farm was also bombed, but no damage was done. We went to view the bomb craters and noticed two small holes in the ground. About two days later they turned out to be time bombs, exploding one afternoon (but without damage).

One of this neighbour's sons had a car on the farm, and one day I was allowed to drive it along a farm road. From then on I wanted to be a racing driver. It was the first time I had ever driven a car. What desires it fomented in me! The next time I drove anything was a Bren Gun carrier in the army!

My half-brother, Pip, (same mother but different father) had a tremendous personality. He had a difficult life - losing his father when a very young boy, then having to cope with a stepfather who was not the easiest person to live with. Pip was a man of great physical and mental courage, a man to admire indeed. He was educated at Ellesmere College and, when at about sixteen years old, he was injured in the leg whilst playing rugby. I cannot recall the name of his injury accurately – osteo-something-or-other – but it affected him for the rest of his life, despite many operations. He had to keep a hole open in his leg to drain out the suppurating infection inside. Every morning he had to dress the leaking wound with an Elastoplast dressing to absorb the leaking fluid and collect bits of bone. This went on for seventy years or more.

Pip had a Mastoid operation which I remember as an operation "within less than an inch from his brain". This expression always impressed me. Being in the thirties, it was held to be a very dangerous operation indeed. He also had an operation on his right arm which resulted in him being unable to straighten it out completely. He had emphysema and had to have a tube put into his lung to drain it. I remember Mother being called to the hospital early in the morning, before light, and before we had a car, so we had to harness the cob to the trap. She was called out because his other lung had begun to collapse but then, suddenly, his sick other lung started to function again. This was in Gobowen hospital, a place where fresh air was a key element in patient recovery, the wards being open to the elements. Once when I went to visit him there was snow on the end of his bed. Tough!

Snakes Alive

When his leg problem was first diagnosed, he walked with a leg iron. It was hurtful to see him limping with this leg, a fit young man inhibited in his movements by this contraption. He used to have to travel in a 'Bath Chair' – a wicker bed on wheels – on which he had to lie if he wanted to get out of the house. I spent a lot of time wheeling him along the lanes around Old Marton and became very fond of him, having great admiration for his fortitude. We used to play a dangerous game by aiming his bed down a slope in the road and letting it go – 'hands off'. It careered down the road with Pip clutching the sides for dear life, but he never came to grief. He had to be pushed up the hill again, full of relief. Through these sorts of escapades we became especially fond of each other – a different relationship than other members of the family had.

One of his more famous pranks was his 'revenge' attack on Canadian cousin Pat Broughall. She was a prankster herself with a tremendous sense of fun and humour, albeit a bit 'nasty' at times! Sugar was rationed but for a prank she put salt in our sugar bowl thus ruining a whole quantity of this scarce commodity. She was staying at our cousin Peter Humphries' house at New Marton, less than a mile away.

Pip decided to take revenge for what he saw as a heinous attack on our meagre sugar ration; he went to New Marton in a winter's evening and climbed up the outside wall to Pat's bedroom. The wall was covered in thick ivy, thus enabling him to get into her bedroom in the dark evening without being seen. He took with him some holly leaves and put them in her bed. Being Pat, she jumped enthusiastically into bed and got thoroughly scratched. She was furious and threw them out of bed. Next morning she jumped out of bed and landed on the holly leaves severely scratching herself again. Then on her dressing table she found a note which read, "Revenge is sweet, Flannel Foot!" She kept a blood-stained holly leaf in a matchbox for a long time.

He had a big problem with sleep-walking. As youngsters we shared a bedroom at Old Marton. We had no electricity so we used candles to take us to bed. One night, at two in the morning, he was woken up with his bed on fire. In his sleep he'd lit a candle and put it under the bed... with hot consequences!

Another funny memory of Pip's sleep-walking was to do with the dairy. As dairy farmers we all called our cows to come into the shippon for milking. You had to raise your voice and call them. We all had our own recognisable calls. When I was working for a neighbouring farmer at Great Fernhill Farm (near Gobowen, about a mile away), I recall him saying to Pip that he could set his clock when he heard me calling the cows in for milking at ten to six in the morning. Not at six o'clock – I was too well trained by my father to be even five minutes late. We had sash windows in our bedroom, and at four o'clock some mornings I remember Pip leaning out of the upstairs window and calling the cows in for milking at the top of his voice. He would never waken up whilst doing this.

Despite all his disabilities, Pip played rugby for Oswetry, even captaining the side, until he broke his nose whilst playing. He also played cricket for Whittington and won 'The Bat' a number of times. It was awarded to the best batsman of the year and was donated by the Rogers family from Rhodesia, formerly of Hindford, the home of the notorious gambler Jack Mytton. Pip was a first class dairy farmer and earned his money despite his physical limitations. Eventually his herd was affected by the foot and mouth epidemic. Our second-born son (who arrived after Terry's death) was born on Pip's birthday; so we named him Edward Philip after Pip.

My father had come from Bath after the First World War. Living on a neighbouring farm to Old Marton, he was fond of teaching agriculture to young men who would come to the farm and live in. He was paid to do this. One of them, a Harry Thornton, married my cousin Joan Davies and they farmed in Cheshire. Harry found a farm near to him for Pip to start his farming career. This was at the beginning of the war, Pip being physically unable to serve in the armed forces.

One pupil came and stayed with us in Rhodesia, bringing his wife and four children with him. He worked in Malawi as an Agricultural Advisory Officer. (He worked at Old Marton during the war, I think.) I remember well that he had a small motor bike which we all craved to ride, and he kindly allowed us to do so.

An interesting thing happened on a neighbouring farm. The farmer, Mr Lawrence, sowed agricultural salt on a ten acre field and had an amazing result. Mushrooms grew everywhere. You could hardly put your foot anywhere without crushing a mushroom. (When I was on leave from the army in 1944, my father took me down there since the field was next to one of ours. The field was in sight of the Lawrences' house, and before we had been there for long, one of the sons appeared at one end of the field carrying a rifle. They were plagued with poachers, people of the 'lower division'.)

They made a fortune (by our standards) by selling the mushrooms in Oswestry. They dumped their pickings in a corner of the field by a gate and then shovelled them into a trailer and sold them without any sophisticated packaging. When we picked mushrooms on our own farm we treated them as if they were gold dust. In all they made £400 which the farmer gave to his four children. This was a lot of money, tax free. If my father made £400 profit in a year he was doing well. Mr Lawrence could neither read nor write but he knew how to farm; one of his daughters kept the books and signed the cheques after her mother died. No-one else ever had the same results since many emulated the Lawrence's example without success, including my father. Agricultural salt sales reached an all time high!

(One of the sons, Gordon, was so cross with one of his sheep dogs he threw his stick at it. It went straight through its body and killed it on the spot.)

At Old Marton we had no electricity so had no hot water in taps – that is, before we had an AGA stove installed, and then it was only for internal use, not on the shed outside. This made clothes washing difficult, and we had to use the copper boiler for hot water. Mother washed by hand every Monday, her only mechanical aid being a 'dolly' and a 'wringer'. The wringer was used to squeeze out the water from the clothes. It had two rollers and a handle to turn them so that the washing moved between the rollers; these were sprung so that they kept an even pressure on the wet clothes. The dolly was used to stir the washing in a metal bath. It could hardly be called a mechanical aid since it was hand powered. It consisted of a stool with five short legs underneath and a long handle above with a cross piece at the top. You held the dolly by hand, pushed it into the bath full of clothes and twisted it back and forth to stir the clothes to clean them. This back-breaking job was done by the ladies whilst we were all at school.

The clothes were hung on a long line in a nearby field for the wind to blow on them and dry them. On wet days the clothes were hung in the kitchen on a specially designed rack, with three bars, operated by a pulley to raise or lower it. The pulley was lowered to a convenient height and the clothes distributed over the parallel bars. It was then raised to a correct height in front of the kitchen grate where the heat was. It was this grate that was used for cooking so it was a great inconvenience to mother who had a large family to feed. The clothes could be there for hours getting dry. Just think of the ironing too, all done with irons heated on the grate which had to be kept almost roaring hot.

My one personal memory of Mondays was that we always had rice pudding since it could be put in the oven whilst the washing was being done. Sometimes for variation we would have tapioca pudding. I hated both! As I remember, we had too much sympathy for mother to complain.

All lighting in winter was by means of paraffin lamps, the glasses of which had to be cleaned every day and the paraffin checked. Lighting them was an art because they shed their light by a very delicate mantle which, when installed, would disintegrate at the slightest touch.

We kept two hives of bees and harvested a considerable amount of honey each year. We loved to eat the combs when they were full of honey whenever they were available. We very rarely got stung since we had adequate bee-proof clothing. Handling the bee hives was a job I enjoyed, especially putting in the queen excluder. This was a device to stop the queen from entering the honey-producing box (called a 'super') so that she could lay her eggs only in the 'brooder' box. The queen was bigger than the other bees so the excluder holes were too small for her to pass through.

When we judged the super to be full of honey and ready to be harvested we put a bee excluder between the super and the rest of the hive so that it was without bees and we could take it away. The bee excluder allowed the bees to leave the super but not return. When a super was full of honey it was removed, an empty one was put in its place and the bee excluder removed. Either an old frame which had just been emptied of its honey and which the bees only had to clean up or an artificial frame which had never been used before was used for the bees to build their honey-carrying cells. I cannot explain the mathematics of it, but the artificial frame carrying the material for cell building had two sides to it and it was a mathematical miracle for the bees to build one cell back to back with another and not waste space. In winter we fed them with sugar and a little water because there were no flowers for them to feed from.

Bird life was plentiful. We had a rookery close by, and every evening flocks of rooks, crows and jackdaws flew past the house on their way to roost. Swallows and swifts built their mud nests under the eaves and in sheds and brought up their young under our noses. Sparrows and starlings also nested everywhere. Robins and wrens were numerous as well as plovers, chaffinches, curlews, corncrakes and swans at certain times of the year. On the watering ponds we had coots and waterhens ('watties'). We were adept at taking wattie hens' eggs. Mother would hard boil them and we would eat them with our bacon and eggs for breakfast.

We always had cuckoos around too, as well as snipe, wood pigeons and owls. These were the noisiest birds at night – the screech owl living up to its name with its appalling screech in a pear tree at night beside the house.

At the bottom of the yard we had a pond which watered the dairy cows, horses, geese and ducks. (A goose was my favourite bird for Christmas lunch.) Every winter it froze over and we had to cut holes in the ice with an axe to water the animals. It froze over enough for us to skate on it, but one day Pip got too adventurous and the ice gave way under him. He nearly drowned. He had difficulty in getting out because he could not heave himself onto solid ice; it simply gave way under him. None of us ventured to help him since the ice would have given way under us too. Eventually he made it to the water's edge and got out – but frozen stiff.

During holidays in the war years, we had three children staying with us since their father, a doctor, had died. They were Tony, Greta and Joe Blackstock – Joe being the youngest and my age. I never followed up their lives when they left school so I have no idea what happened to them. They were good for games during the holidays when we were not working on the farm. I can only presume my parents were well paid for their trouble since having three more mouths to feed during the war was quite a commitment.

As well as the Blackstocks, we were allocated two children refugees from London who complained bitterly that their milk in London came out of lovely clean bottles and not "out of these dirty cows"! They stayed about a year.

We also had two Italian prisoners of war staying at Old Marton who were declared safe and co-operative. They were dressed in prisoner of war clothes and were allowed to walk the countryside without supervision. Their clothes were of a special colour with a round patch of a different colour on the back. We became quite friendly with them. One of them managed to father a child in the district. I suppose some ladies thought they were macho men being continentals. We all tried frantically to learn Italian and to teach them English so conversations in the house were a mixture of us all trying to show off our knowledge of one language or the other, punctuating our speech with Italian words or phrases. We made every effort to sound continental by imitating their accent but with little success. If we did manage something we were soon shouted down as being show offs. They were sailors off an Italian cruiser and had the most atrocious table manners. And, of course, they worked on the farm.

Guy Fawkes Night always brought us happiness because a man used to bring us fireworks. We had jumping jacks, Catherine wheels, rockets, sparklers and many other exciting things, but there was also a danger of a rocket flying over the house and landing in the stackyard, where all the winter hay and corn was stored. We always made sure it was pointed away from the buildings, putting it into a bottle to limit its trajectory. I don't know who the man was, but my parents must have had a hand in the arrangements somewhere.

At Christmas time, a man came round every year to sing carols for money, going from farm to farm. He was known as "old jy" as he always sang, "comfot and jy".

During the winter our wheat and oats harvest had to be threshed. This was done by a threshing machine drawn by a steam engine which went from farm to farm. Certain men followed the machine as it was an annual form of income. They were called 'mourners', somewhat obviously.

Being the youngest in the family I was given the worst job, which was to keep the steam engine full of water. It had to be carried by buckets from the nearby pond and poured into a drum. As soon as the drum was full and you thought you could have a rest, the engine driver, a very nice man, would suck it all into his boiler and I would have to start the thankless task of filling it again. It was impossible not to get soaked, usually in atrocious weather. At least that's what I thought of it! Much pleading with Father to let someone else do it never achieved anything since we all had our jobs to do and mine was deemed the easiest and therefore fit for the youngest to do.

Feeding the sheaves into the threshing drum, rotating at high speed, was a skilled job as each sheaf had to have its string cut and then be handed to the man feeding the drum. This feeding had to be done expertly in order not to clog up the drum with too much corn at a time, thus preventing a proper cleaning of each sheaf. This went on for hours – never a moment wasted – hour after hour for two days or more, sometimes three. We needed string to tie up the sacks of grain coming out of the other end of the machine, the box. It was the responsibility of the man cutting the twine on the sheaf to find the knot and cut it at that point; otherwise it could not be used to tie the sacks of grain. It had to be so; the string could not be threaded through the bagging needle if it had a knot halfway down.

One other point in this regard was that sheaves of corn also carried thistles as well as stalks of grain. It was a painful job feeding the sheaf into the spinning drum; it had to be fed in evenly otherwise the grain could not be threshed out. You could always hear when a sheaf was fed in too quickly as the even hum of the drum would alter drastically. Everyone would be ready to comment on the lack of skill of the drum feeder that day. Brother Tom would be picking thistle-thorns out of his hands for days.

Mother had to feed everyone for lunch including the mourners. Their clothes were so dirty that she put newspapers on the tables instead of tablecloths. The men never objected; it saved them from feeling guilty for dirtying her tablecloths. We had the same threshing team for many years, the leader being a fine man named Joe.

Joe graduated from driving a steam engine to a huge tractor called a Minneapolis Moline. Its wheels were higher than me. It had to pull three machines at a time through the country lanes: the threshing box (a huge machine), a baler and a tying machine to tie bundles of straw. The straw was used as bedding for cattle in sheds. When I look back on it, the skills we kids had at a very early stage were amazing – and we received no pay!

It was part of our life and we never expected anything. For example, milking by hand or by milking machine was just accepted as part of our daily lives

When I visited my old school after I had left, one older master, Mr Felton, said he had always admired my parents for teaching us how to work.

Some dreadfully, excruciatingly tedious jobs we had to do as kids were 'cocking' hay and 'stooking' corn sheaves ('shocks'). We couldn't argue with our Father; we just did it – all day, every day, with no pay. We knew no other way of living; it was normal country living and we expected nothing else. It was expected of every farmer's son. What eased the agony was the knowledge that there was nothing else to do to make you yearn you were somewhere else – no TV, no sport, etc., to make you wish you were there watching or playing. Life in the thirties was so different to that experienced by today's generation.

Hay was cut in a field specially set apart for that purpose, meaning cattle were not allowed to graze it down. It grew to maybe four feet high and was then cut by a mowing machine drawn by two horses. The grass fell in even swaths and was left to dry for a day or two, after which it was turned over by a 'turner' drawn by one horse. It was a cleverly designed machine as it picked up the swath and neatly turned it over for the other side to dry. Another type of machine to do the same sort of job was called a 'tedder' – different in construction but able to turn over a swath of hay.

When father deemed it was ready, it was raked into lines by a machine drawn by one horse. It brought the grass into more concentrated lines and we kids had to go and create 'cocks' shaped like inverted egg cups. Every bit of hay had to be handled with a 'pikel' - a long-handled two pronged fork. A most tedious job – hour after hour, often in hot sunshine and your work could be seen for its professionalism by all who walked by. Every cock had to be so constructed that it made the rain drain down the side and not enter its centre. Often the hay was baled in the field, and this required a different process altogether.

Corn 'shocking' was different and had to be done by pairs of workers. Corn was cut by a 'binder' drawn by three horses – two abreast and one in front. The binder was a heavy machine and needed strong Shire horses for the job. The two horses abreast were controlled by a driver sitting on the binder, but the lead horse had to be ridden. That was often my job which I loved. The back of the horse was so broad you could not put a saddle on it so I always sat on a sack. It was a skilful job even for a youngster as the lead horse had to be kept at a definite distance from the edge of the standing corn and turning at the end of a run needed skill and attention. It reminds me of the skill needed to turn a span of sixteen trek-oxen at the headland when ploughing in Rhodesia.

It was heavy work for the hoses, which had to be rested frequently to catch their breath, because of the hard work they put in. Their nostrils would flare as they were rested to get their breath back.

The cut corn went through the binder and came out as tied sheaves or 'shocks', each shock (sheaf) being ejected when the right amount of corn stalks had accumulated. The sheaf was tied with binder twine, a coarse brownish string made for the purpose. The knot on the sheaf was tied by an ingenious device; it tied the knot and then cut the twine before it was ejected from the binder. Naturally, as they were ejected they fell in lines, and this is where we came in the next day and 'stooked' them in sixes. Two people faced each other, leaning one shock against another, forming a shape like the apex of a pyramid, putting six sheaves together. This was called a 'stook'. So our job today was to go 'stooking'.

After a week or so, depending on the weather, they had to be turned so that the inside became outside for complete drying. Often a corn field would have been undersown with grass and clover seed and the early growth would have been cut by the binder. Thus the lower part of the cut sheaf would contain green, wet grass, and this had to be dried even though the cut corn was dry. The job took time and this explains why the stook had to be turned.

The binder mechanics were driven by a large wheel which was hidden in the centre of the machine. The machine balanced on the wheel and left a distinct mark on the soil. This was our guide for stooking and is why you would see perfectly symmetrical lines of stooks in a field – always a pleasant sight to a farmer, showing order and symmetry. I always enjoyed the sight, anyway, having been the author of much of it.

The next operation was to cart the corn to the stackyard on wagons drawn by horses. (Today, of course, harvesting is done by a combine and all that I have described has disappeared from the modern farming programme.) This harvesting was nearly always done during hot weather, and Father slaked the men's thirst with cider. It was stored in barrels in the cellar of the house to keep cool and was carried to the field, when needed, in 'noggins'. Noggins were wicker-covered ceramic containers (demijohns); we called them 'firkins' in Africa.

I was once sent to the house to refill the containers so on the way back to the field I had a swig (a sample taste) of the cider and probably displayed evidence of my 'theft'! Thereafter I became known as Noggin Neddy!

It was a tradition for the farm workers to come into the kitchen for a couple of beers, or cider if preferred, on Christmas Eve. Drink was never an issue in our house although I used to take a swig of neat gin if I could find an open bottle and wondered what people could see in it. Mother said Father had had "too much to drink" as he celebrated the birth of his twins. That was the only reference made concerning drinking. I never saw my father or anyone else in the family the worse for wear.

A farming neighbour was a tippler, and I used to hate going into his house in case he had had too much to drink. I was afraid of him although nothing untoward ever happened. His son was a groomsman at my sister's wedding.

One joke was played on Tom by my father. He was sent to this neighbour for "a tin of elbow grease" which Tom hurried to collect. He came back red-faced.

Our neighbour on the other side had a son of about twenty who suddenly died of TB. The first we knew about it was when we heard a car coming racing down the drive at ten o'clock at night, honking its horn furiously. It was the dead man's sister calling for help as their phone was out of order and they wanted to call the doctor. It was too late, but the doctor came anyway and certified him dead from natural causes. Mother went to the family next day and 'laid him out' (that is, she washed him and cleaned up the mess in the bed in which he had died – blood and excreta etc – as he had bled to death. This was an accepted practice in the farming community. Death was not a problem to that generation. When Mother's father died, his body was put in the lounge of their home and all the children were expected to kiss their dead father good morning every day until he was buried.

Snakes Alive

5

Sandhurst and India

I had a favourite cousin, John Davies, who lived in Whittington with his widowed mother, my aunty Mary, and his sister, Joan (who married Harry Thornton, mentioned previously). I never knew John's father; he must have died when I was very young. We used to go and stay with Aunty Mary and go to school from there. My abiding memory of these visits was that she made lumpy porridge. It was not part of her diet so she was unpractised at the art of making the smooth porridge we were used to. She only made it for our benefit, knowing it was part of our breakfast at Old Marton.

John could do nothing wrong in my eyes. Whatever he did, I wanted to do too. He qualified as a Surveyor and Estate Agent in a company called CE Williams & Co in Oswestry and became a partner. I wanted to follow in his footsteps so when I left school I was articled to do the same thing in the same company. He joined the army and was commissioned into the Royal Welch Fusiliers and rose to the rank of Major. He was killed in France in 1943. He had married a lovely lady named Wendy but had had no children.

The owner of the company was a Bernie Williams who had been badly injured by a shell in the First World War; thirty years later he was still shedding bits of shrapnel from his hands onto his desk blotter. He died of pneumonia in 1943 whilst I was working there.

Because I was not in a reserved occupation (and before I could be called up) I volunteered for the army and joined the Royal Engineers. This was a deliberate ploy because they trained recruits in surveying, which was my dream. It did not succeed because I had not been articled long enough to qualify. I was trained in explosives, laying land mines and building Bailey Bridges. We loved it!

After further training as a despatch rider on motorbikes and in Bren gun carriers, flame throwers and machine guns carried on Bren gun carriers, destruction of bridges, railway lines, buildings, using mortars and other army hardware, I was put forward for a commission.

I was commissioned at the Royal Military College at Sandhurst. We had an amusing incident whilst training. We were confronted by a deep trench with some ropes and timber of various length and shapes. The instructor said this was a bottomless pit and we had to use the ropes and timber to cross it. One enterprising cadet (for that is what we were) tied a piece of rope to a timber, let it down into the trench, used it to clamber down to the bottom and then climbed up the other side. The instructor remonstrated with him, but the cadet countered by saying, "Sir, if this is a bottomless pit then *this* is an endless rope." He got away with his joke.

I remember the final assault course we did before we were commissioned. It was a mile obstacle course with every kind of wicked obstacle you could imagine! It began with us wading through a lake which was iced over. The water was so deep it came up to my neck, and I had to break the ice with my Adam's apple! One of our company was so short we had to hold his rifle above our heads, and he clung on to it for dear life! Strangely enough I remember his surname was Middleton – 'Middy' to us.

We were taught to keep our head dry to protect ourselves from the cold. This was a laugh. Our obstacle course equipment (battle dress) included a knapsack which was tightly strapped to our back to stop it bouncing around. When wading through the lake it obviously got filled with water. The first obstacle after the lake was a high wall which you had to roll over to present as little a profile to the enemy as possible, keeping your head down. The result was that the water in the knapsack poured into your helmet, soaking head and shoulders if they were not already soaked. So much for keeping your head dry!

I was awarded the Belt, the second highest honour the College could award to each intake. (My son, Brian, was awarded the equivalent honour when trained as an officer in the Rhodesian army.) My Canadian cousin,

Sandhurst and India

Pat Broughall, who was commissioned into the Auxiliary Territorial Service, the ATS, was at my passing out parade and "nearly passed out with pride", so she says. I knew nothing of the award beforehand. She went back to her barracks and wrote a marvellous letter to my parents, dated 19 April 1945 or "The Day". I still have the Medallion and the letter. In it Pat speaks of me having in my hat a whole "eiderdown of feathers"!

Here are the relevant parts of the letter, now over sixty five years old:

> *Isn't it absolutely splendid of Ted to win the Medallion. I am so excited, it was so thrilling to hear Field Marshal Sir Alan Brooke say, "For the most outstanding improvement on the course, the Medallion is awarded to Officer Cadet E Nicholas." Ted practically gaped and shouted, "Sir." I nearly fainted with excitement.*
>
> *He came through the ranks and gave a smashing salute to the G.O.C. Home Forces who shook his hand and said some nice words. Ted saluted and marched back to his place as if winning the Royal Military College medal was a routine job like going up to the pay table for a week's pay!*
>
> *It really is a whole eiderdown of feathers in Ted's cap to be awarded the Medallion and anyone not acquainted with the RMC and the present OCTU[1] training would not appreciate the triumph of it.*
>
> *After the awards, the Companies marched to the rear of the parade square, Ted and the belt dropping out of position and slow marching singly at the end, each of them giving Brooke a salute as they passed. I was almost collapsing with pride.*
>
> *After the award and the parade was moving to the arrear of the parade square, Ted's platoon commander Capt. Healey cane and spoke to me. He said all sorts of nice things about Ted but I was far too excited to remember them. We stood together watching Ted do the slow march up the steps, in the place of honour, behind the rest of the company, Ted, the Belt*

---

[1] OCTU means Officer Cadet Training Unit

and the Adjutant on his horse. The Belt is considered the first award; the Medallion is a totally different award and just as pride making!

I waited with Fred's wife until Ted had changed and we went to the NAAFI[2] for some coffee. Ted came there looking like a million dollars in his new uniform. He was besieged with congratulations and hearty backslaps. We walked back to the road and hopped in a taxi, me hopping out at the mess. Oh how I wish you could have been there, it is such an impressive ceremony.

Of course Ted will have told you all about this (does his cap still fit!?) but even if you had been there you couldn't have glowed with more pride than I did.

Love,

Pat

Because it was wartime, the peacetime award of the Sword of Honour was reduced to being called the Belt (a sword was not manufactured during wartime). The Belt was a Sam Browne leather belt worn by officers. This was now awarded to the cadet who should have had the Sword of Honour. The peacetime Belt now became the Medallion, the award given to me.

My father, who was a Sergeant Major in the First World War in India, was of course very proud of his son and kept hold of the medal and letter until he died. Only then did I hold it myself, after my mother came out to Rhodesia in 1972.

I was posted to India in 1945 and travelled on the French luxury liner (now a troop ship) the Ile de France, which took us to Bombay. I was then posted to the 5th Royal Ghurkha Rifles (Frontier Force) stationed at Abbottabad in the North West Frontier Province, now part of Pakistan. We travelled by train for seven days to get there, going via Delhi. It was close to the Chinese border, and it was alternately stinking hot or freezing cold.

---

[2] NAAFI means Navy Army Air Force Institute, a place to buy tea and cakes

Sandhurst and India

I was not yet twenty years old and was not a seasoned soldier. One of the first things I experienced there was the visit of a pack of jackals at night. A pack of about fifty, now in their white winter coats, would gather outside my cottage and howl in unison with the most appalling cacophony of noise. Sleep was impossible.

A snake charmer (or so he called himself through an interpreter) offered to clear my garden of snakes. This was a fair offer; I knew nothing of the snake culture but was glad I could be rid of them even though I had never seen one. He 'caught' three snakes within a few yards of my cottage, and to this day I don't know how he did it. He stalked slowly around the garden with his head cocked on one side, as if listening for something, then occasionally dashed into some bushes and flowers and came out brandishing a snake. He did this three times as if listening or waiting for some revelation. I don't know what kind of snakes he caught, but I was assured by the interpreter that I had been saved from some deadly creatures. I think he popped them into a basket from which, I am sure, he had brought them.

It was obvious he had planted the snakes there but they did not glide away. Why, I don't know, but I had to pay him a handsome reward in rupees with the hidden threat that if I didn't, more snakes would come back in greater numbers and I could even find one in my bed! It was obviously a well-practised hoax with the interpreter playing a very co-operative role. The charmer had put the snakes there earlier, so I believe. It has always baffled me why the snakes stayed in one place instead of gliding away, which any sensible snake would do whilst he went through his routine. I saw the last snake he 'found' curled up in the shape of a ring; it made no effort to escape when he 'caught' it. I never saw another snake in that area again, nor ever heard of one, nor did any other officer go through the same experience that I did. The only other snakes I saw were from the basket of a 'snake charmer' in Bombay. He had a cobra, obviously de-fanged, which came out of his basket with its hood up. The charmer thought it was not displaying itself enough so he kept on poking it with his hand under its hood to make it rise up higher.

Another one had a tame mongoose and he offered to let us see it fight with a snake. We had to throw him cash, and when the bounty stopped flowing he took out a snake from his basket and then let the mongoose loose. It rushed at the snake and bit its head off before the snake could attack its enemy. It was not one of the more expensive cobras!

Abbottabad was a garrison town, its economy much enhanced by the presence of various regiments of troops. In 1945, it had no special features; it was just a small, insignificant place. Its military significance was that it was there to monitor the Kyber Pass – the connection and trade route between India and Afghanistan – to stop infiltration between the two countries. That is why my regiment was designated 'Frontier Force', signifying our calling so as not to be confused with the other Ghurkha regiments.

The Ghurkha's traditional weapon was the 'kukri', which was issued to every Ghurkha officer. I still have mine somewhere in Shropshire. It was a fantastically sharp and balanced knife used for chopping wood etc. as well as for killing people. In Nepal they had a much larger variety which they used to slaughter cattle with. It was a two handed type, and a young man 'earned his spurs' by cutting off an animal's head with one clean blow.

One story going around was that a Ghurkha soldier fought against a Japanese soldier, hand to hand, slashing out with his kukri. The Jap said, "Ah, missed!" to which the Ghurkha replied, "Wait till you shake your head!"

The dominant tribe in the area – a vast area, it has to be said – were Pathans. They were renowned for their slippery skills. It was claimed they could get into your bedroom at night and take the sheet you were sleeping on from under you whilst you were sleeping. There was a Pathan regiment as part of the garrison in Abbottabad, led by British Army officers. One of them told me a true story of one of their soldiers applying for leave to go into Afghanistan to "deal with" somebody who, he had heard, had insulted his sister. His request was refused, naturally, but he went AWOL anyway. He came back satisfied with his mission and was quite happy to serve a lengthy prison sentence since, to him, tribal and family justice had been satisfied. Not much has changed!

Social life was non-existent. There were no picture houses, dance floors or white girls around us, and it was 'infra dig' to go out with Indian girls. However, one of my friends, Jock Ross, ignored the social stigma of such a liaison and had an Indian girlfriend. What happened between them

Sandhurst and India

I can only guess since they only went out together at night to avoid being seen. Some five years later I met him in Bulawayo, he now being a sergeant in the Rhodesian army, but he didn't remember me.

A romantic event was the marriage of our Adjutant, Capt. George Burt, to Caroline, daughter of the Major General. We were all jealous that he had found someone 'behind our backs' when we had no-one to court. Years later, in 1952, I met Caroline at the Bulawayo racecourse, but she died soon afterwards. I met George in Mutare in 1974, he now being a car salesman for Duly and Co.

In the officers' mess at Abbottabad we played silly games out of boredom. Drinking was quite an occupation although it never got out of hand. Our favourite drink was a 'Gin Piazz', the name meaning 'onion'. You took a champagne glass and put a tot of neat gin in it. You then took three small pickled onions and soaked them in the gin. After a while you took a toothpick, speared an onion and sucked the neat gin out of it. You put it back and speared another one. This went on until your gin was finished; then you ate the onion.

Another drink was a 'Chota Peg' (straight whisky and water). Chota Peg meant 'just a small one' (not a double). Cries of "Chota Peg" could be heard around the mess as orders were passed to mess office waiters.

The craziest game we played in the mess was a classical miniature army battle. We had a large mess lounge, and our game was to overturn a sofa at each end. In the mess we had numerous empty artillery shell cases with complementary dead shells. The trick was to put a small shell in a larger shell case, hide behind the sofa, and then rise up and hurl the shell at the 'enemy'. Accuracy was missing, and many a shell went through a window or through a painting hanging on the wall. Ghurkha messing servants stood around the walls of the mess, taking down the names of culprits. You found a charge for your misdemeanour in your next mess bill. This game was usually instigated after a few Gin Piazzes. It was a dangerous game with huge potential for injuries, but I do not recall anyone being hospitalised.

We had a few Indian officer friends from one of the Indian regiments. One Jemadar (junior officer rank in the Indian army) took a few of us to his family home right against the Chinese border – a walk of about ten miles through totally uninhabited countryside. It was on this journey I saw my first iguana. When we reached his family home and completed the necessary introductions, we were told to rest in a thatched hut on charpoys (Indian beds). When I was lying down and looking up at the thatched roof I saw a krait, one of the deadliest snakes in the world, moving through the thatch. We got out of there smartly! The danger was that the snake could lose its grip on the rafters and fall onto the bed you were lying on. According to the Jemadar, this was not uncommon. We had curried chicken and rice for lunch, and very acceptable it was too. The journey back was long, hot and hard, but we had had a taste of the real India.

My work at the camp was mainly administrative with an emphasis on repatriation of soldiers to Nepal where certain government facilities were available to returning retiring Nepalese soldiers. By this time I could speak Urdu (Hindustani) and was in the process of learning the Nepalese language called Ghurkhali or Kuskura. There was considerable turmoil in the army because independence was looming and the British influence was deliberately being diminished. As a consequence, because of my administrative experience, in early 1946 I was posted to Bombay and was promoted to an Embarkation Staff Officer (ESO) in the Ministry of Transport with the responsibility of embarking and disembarking troops from, or into, troopships. It was a busy time because British troops were leaving India in their hundreds and many Indian troops were returning from overseas duty.

As British soldiers we were not popular and were subject to much verbal abuse. The great Indian cry, whenever they saw British soldiers, was "Jai Hind, Jai Hind" meaning "Victory for India". If a bus happened to pass by they would throw bottles at you and anything else they could find. We did not go out at night unless on duty.

I spent my twenty first birthday in Bombay and was determined not to cower in barracks on such a day. With two other friends we heavily armed ourselves; I had a .45 revolver and a .38, both strapped to my legs for easy access, both fully loaded and ready to fire. I don't know what we expected but we were ready for it. Mother sent me £5 for my birthday, but it never arrived so I had no twenty first birthday present! It was in Bombay that I met Jack's wife's brother; I cannot remember under what circumstances we met, but we had a meal together.

We were not stationed in a regular army camp but in a transformed hotel called 'The Fort'. There were no bar facilities so we had a ration of liquor delivered to us physically every month and debited against our pay. It consisted of whisky, gin and beer, and we spent the month bartering for the liquor we wanted or didn't want. At night, over our liquor, we played cards and music and were generally happy people.

During the day, when off duty, we loved to sit on the sea wall on Marine Drive and drool over the gorgeous wealthy Indian families with the girls wearing beautiful, stunning saris of the most wonderful colours and styles. They were mostly of a group called 'Parsees'. The Parsees were the wealthiest people in Bombay and lived in an area called Malabar Hill. There they built the most expensive and lovely homes. My understanding was that on top of each house they built a grill on which they put their dead relatives for the vultures to clean up the body. I think their religion was akin to the Hindus.

One of the difficulties we had as army officers was being the target of beggars, particularly children, who demanded 'bakshees' (handouts). Children would approach you with shoe polish on their hands and fingers threatening to smear it over your uniform, especially around your crutch when we were wearing khaki shorts. They were so persistent that sometimes we had to deter them until we saw a policeman who would sort them out. Poverty was obvious and rampant. Indian parents would deliberately break their children's limbs when they were babies and set them in grotesquely disfigured shapes to attract the sympathy of adult strangers. Beggars chewed betel leaves which had a narcotic effect but which coloured their mouths and teeth a disgusting red.

In the Hindu religion they believed in re-incarnation and that the spirit of a dead relative could re-appear in a cow or a rat or anything they fancied. Cows particularly were prone to carry spirits of dead relatives and could wander the streets at will.

Bombay had a beautiful shopping area which was particularly attractive after the wartime English scene. I bought my mother a lovely bedside rug which eventually arrived at Old Marton some weeks later. When we went out at night (infrequently, I have to say, because of unnecessary security dangers) it was a great pleasure to see the lighted shops with windows full of expensive goods.

On Saturday afternoons a couple of us went to the Bombay racecourse with a couple of girls from the Convent. One was a beautiful girl called Azan Masters. She was very pale-skinned although not of European descent. Her skin was almost olive-coloured but had a bit of whiteness to it – difficult to describe, but could possibly be described as 'creamy'. A friend said she was of Persian descent, hence the pale skin and the un-Indian surname.

We had an Indian bearer, not a batman, to do our washing and ironing and to clean our room. Starching of our uniforms was done with rice water and very effectively too. The bearer I had was a wonderful man to whom I gave all my pay to look after for me after an occasion when I had had my pocket picked of most of my month's pay.

For a time I had a Jewish girlfriend who had an importing business, and we used to go tooling around Bombay in her car marketing her imports which she stored in a 'Godown' (warehouse) on the dockside. I saw a lot of the city this way as she sold her goods to traders in the suburbs, and I saw much of the poverty unheard of in Europe. It was said that many people were born in a street and never ventured out of it all their lives. They didn't survive; they just died in their poverty where they were born.

Poverty in India was unbelievable, particularly among the 'untouchables' who could practically never find work because of the caste system. They were despised people, treated like animals with no pity, no compassion afforded them.

In Bombay I experienced a dreadful monsoon cyclone. A very serious weather warning was given to all shipping; all ships were advised to leave harbour and ride it out at sea. One ship, the Stirling Castle, one of the Union Castle Line luxury liners but now a troop ship, decided not to go out but stay moored to Ballard Pier, a major mooring place made of wood for the bigger ships but without any inner harbour protection, being exposed almost directly to the sea. She was so hammered by the storm that she nearly battered the pier to pieces. The sky turned absolutely yellow, and rainfall of thirty six inches in twenty four hours was recorded. If you started to cross the street dry and got half way across you would be soaked to the skin, thoroughly drenched before reaching the other side. It was on the Stirling Castle I learned of another drink. It was called an 'Old

Sandhurst and India

Fashioned' and I was taught it by the Purser of that ship whilst working with him on army business. You took a whisky glass, put two teaspoons of sugar in the bottom, added crushed ice (crushed being important) and then filled it with Irish whisky. After a couple of those on an empty stomach before lunch you had trouble walking down the gangway. It carried an unhealthy and unholy punch. I had an army motor cycle to get back and forth from the docks where I worked, and it was a wonder I arrived safely, having to travel through the centre of the city. The food we had was excellent, especially their curry and rice. I have never eaten better.

Just before I got to Bombay an ammunition ship blew up in the harbour, and a two ton piece of sheet steel from the side of the ship was blown for more than a mile, landing on the doorstep of Barclays Bank in the main street. Great damage was done to the harbour, and it took years to repair. In Rhodesia, I was amazed to meet, in Somabula, a farmer who had been in the British Army and was there at the time.

Snakes Alive

6

Last Days in England

I left India in February 1947 and arrived at Southampton on the coldest day they had had in fifty years. After Bombay, I was frozen! It took me nearly two days to reach Old Marton because of snow and ice on the railway lines. For my Jewish girlfriend in Bombay I agreed to take some goods to her family in London. They put me up for the night, but I still struggled to get home. Getting off the train at Welsh Frankton station I swore with every step that I took that at the first opportunity I would go back to India. I loved the place and had a girlfriend there anyway.

At home I was so cold I used to eat in the kitchen, the warmest room in the house, with one hand in my pocket to keep it warm. Bye and bye I would change hands.

I went back to my regiment in Crickhowell in South Wales – after ten days instead of seven days' disembarkation leave because we were snowed in – and was immediately posted to Germany. Whilst sitting on the train to take me home for a week's embarkation leave, an orderly came and took me back to my regiment because orders had been changed; I was to go to the Royal Artillery Regiment at Clatterbridge, near Birkenhead. I was furious and sulked for days!

At Clatterbridge I was given the jobs of camp Messing Officer and Messing Officer of the Officers' Mess – both jobs I thoroughly hated. I was an infantry officer, not some desk-bound administrative idiot. Serves me right for sulking! One amusing incident occurred at the Officers' Mess. I apparently was always bragging about the strength of the curry and rice I was used to in India. The cooks decided to give me a lesson and test me, with the object of dampening my ardour and my criticism of their curry. So the next time we had curry they deliberately spiked my plate with neat curry powder, about five times the strength of the rest. Now they swear this was true, but I never noticed it so their trick fell flat and they agreed my bragging had substance!

I had a big problem with the CO, a Lt Colonel. It was the duty of every company, first thing every morning, to advise me as Messing Officer the number of soldiers under their command that day so that I could order the necessary rations. When all the information was at hand I would send a written order with a driver and a three ton truck to the army depot in Liverpool and collect the amount of rations as indicated by my order. This was a routine matter, and we never had problems until one day no one told me the Colonel was returning that day with a bunch of troops from an exercise which he had been conducting, outside the camp and some miles away. I got the information, quite by chance at about 10am, when I should have had it before 8am. I immediately sent a truck back to Liverpool, but they were closed and refused to give me more rations.

I dished up a somewhat meagre meal and had many complaints. These reached the Colonel's ears and he was furious. He would not accept my explanation, and he 'gave me the gears' as we would say. I never had good communications with him even until my tour of duty was over. One complaint that day was that there was insufficient sugar in the coffee. He demanded a cup of the coffee and was taken aback when he could find nothing wrong with it. The wind was taken completely out of his sails and he had a somewhat guilty, shamefaced look on his face – not that he would admit it.

The head cook told me later that he had heard the complaint and had dumped a whole packet of sugar into the coffee container just before the Colonel had tested it, thank goodness! It took the edge off his fury, but I was never accepted in his eyes again. He was an Artillery man and I was an Infantry officer – 'never the twain shall meet'. I was used to crawling through ditches and hedges and trenches and not comfortable being behind the front, firing shells at the enemy miles out if sight. I think professionally we looked down on each other.

Last Days in England

One of our officers, a captain, used to leave the mess early each evening and go to write to his wife every day. What love; what an example!

The camp was large and was the Brigade Headquarters. Despite what the Colonel thought of me I was acceptable to the Brigadier, a very fine soldier, and took him (or, at least, he took me) to Old Marton to collect some farm produce: eggs, homemade butter, dressed poultry, ducks and so on – all of which were in short supply, probably even illegal to sell privately. This was in late 1947, and it was all for his personal consumption. My father let me down horribly when he asked the Brigadier when I was going to be promoted to Captain. I hurriedly explained that as I was soon to be de-mobbed it was not worth promoting me. It sounded as if we were bribing the Brigadier with our produce.

I changed jobs and was involved in radar. The object was to track incoming enemy aircraft and train the anti-aircraft guns onto them. We had two types of radar equipment: one which picked up an enemy aircraft 120 miles away but which was not linked to the guns, and another which spotted an aircraft 60 miles away. It was this one that reported information to the guns in detail and which we used to train the guns on the incoming aircraft. The first set was used to warn the second set from which direction to expect the enemy. After a while, when I became proficient, I was sent to Kidlington near Oxford on a special mission, much to the Colonel's delight, I am sure. The Air Force was testing a new bombsight, and our job was to track the aircraft carrying the new sight so that at any given second the designers could calculate the height, speed and direction the aircraft was travelling at the moment the bomb was released. An exacting job, but my team became very proficient and we had good success. Our tour of duty lasted three weeks, and then we handed over to another team. These men were so badly trained that I phoned our Brigade Major and told him the whole exercise would collapse if they took charge. I was due for de-mob that week, but I agreed to stay on and train the newcomers. A major from the regiment of the incoming team was sent to beef up the newcomers and make sure they did their job. The Brigade Major agreed to delay my de-mob for a couple of weeks, and when I got back to Clatterbrige I was greeted with his statement, "I believe we covered ourselves with glory" – the only complement I had ever received since leaving Sandhurst. I was probably not a very good soldier although I tried to be because I enjoyed the army. I was de-mobbed in early 1948. A year later I was out of the country thus fulfilling my desire never to stay in the country longer than absolutely necessary.

Now I had to start civilian life again and it took me some time to adjust. There was no need for me on my father's farm so what was there for me to do? There was no money to start me off on something, and the thought of being cooped up in a university for some years was beyond me to contemplate. I had no desire for such a life, and what was I to study anyway? I had no academic qualifications and no clear ambition. My pre-war desire to be a surveyor and estate agent had dried up. I mooched around for some weeks feeling quite miserable and regretting the day I had left the army. I should have applied for a permanent commission and made the army my career. I loved it but it was too late now.

Pip came to my rescue, and I went to work for him. He had run a fifty-nine acre farm in Cheshire but now decided to move to Great Fernhill Farm near Gobowen, a couple of miles from Old Marton. It was no long term solution but it was a start. His new farm was a hundred and ninety five acres, a big jump from his previous fifty-nine and involved purchasing many more dairy cows – mainly Ayrshires – and equipment. From what he told me he paid cash for everything, a sure sign of his farming ability.

When we were in full swing it was my job every morning to call the cows in for milking. My father had trained us to be very careful that we kept to schedule in everything we did. At Old Marton, evening milking was at four o'clock, not five past. It was here we learned how to drink hot tea from a saucer when time for milking was running out.

So at Fernhill I was always on time, calling the cows in at exactly ten to six for milking at six. Many years later a close-by farmer told me he heard me calling the cows and set his watch by it. What horrified me was that he had heard me about a mile away.

It was at this time that the direction of my life took a permanent turn. Mother went to school with a local Hindford family named Rogers. This family emigrated to Southern Rhodesia and did very well. The oldest member was Uncle Bert – no blood relative but that was what we called him. He had been a blacksmith in the Boer War and had stayed on when the war was over. He was a great cattle man and had started trading in native cattle in Southern Rhodesia, in the Tuli Block in the lowveld, which was lion country. He was also a great horseman and had travelled the district on horseback. He had many tales of brushes with lions. For example, one day, his horse refused to go any further towards a river which Uncle Bert was going to use to water his horse. Realising something unusual was up he dismounted and crept up to the river. There he saw three lions at the water's edge, and he shot all three. I'm sure the story is true because he was not a man to draw attention to himself and in later years was a fine man to work for.

He had a bit of money in Hindford where the family was born. He used this and became very successful. He held the trading rights for the area and made a fortune through his cattle trading and store which he had built at West Nicholson and is there to this day. He was known among the Africans for his honesty.

West Nicholson was bordered by the Umzingwane river which had a huge catchment area stretching right back to Bulawayo about a hundred and fifty miles away. It flowed into the Limpopo above Beitbridge, the border post between Rhodesia and South Africa, and then on to the Pacific Ocean at Lourenco Marques, now Maputo, in Mozambique.

At West Nicholson, the river was about a hundred yards wide and sometimes came down in a massive flood which cut off traffic to and from South Africa. There was no bridge there, only a low level road (basically in sand) and traffic could be held up for a couple of days. A permanent rope bridge was thrown up for pedestrians, but no vehicular traffic could move. The store was within a hundred yards of the river so much shopping was done on these occasions. Trek-oxen were on stand-by to drag out any unfortunate vehicle which got stuck in the floodwaters – a wise investment! Many years later a high level bridge was constructed and such conditions no longer prevailed. It was christened "Rogers Bridge", named after Uncle Bert (whose surname was Rogers).

He bought twenty-five thousand acres at West Nicholson and another twenty-five thousand acres at Mchabezi Ranch including Todd's Hotel where the main attraction was a tame giraffe. He also bought a garage in a nearby town, Gwanda, found gold at West Nicholson where he made a fortune, and bought another mine near a village called Colleen Bawn on the road between Gwanda and West Nicholson. Later on at

Heany Junction (some fifteen miles outside Bulawayo) he bought another twenty six thousand acres of land, selling six thousand and retaining a manageable twenty thousand.

Uncle Bert was a great Hereford breeder, so much so that after the war he was invited to judge the Hereford class at the Agricultural Show in Bulawayo. Other than the Rand Easter Show in Johannesburg, it was the premier agricultural show in southern Africa, specialising in cattle. He was a very quiet man, but his wife, Aunty Chips, told me that deep down inside he was "very pleased" to receive the invitation.

As his enterprises grew he brought out his brothers from Hindford: John, Syd and Stan. They formed the company 'Rogers Bros. & Son'. The son was Uncle Bert's only child, Jack, and he inherited all the estate when Uncle Bert died. I think John eventually returned to England. Syd became Tom's godfather and it was he who donated the cricket bat to the Whittington cricket club that Tom won more than once. He died in Capetown as did Uncle Bert. Stan died in Bulawayo.

West Nicholson, Gwanda and their other properties were in the lowveld – always dry and very hot. For those interested in farming, there was a tremendous difference in ranching at West Nicholson and Bulawayo. Bulawayo was at 4250 feet above sea level with a rainfall of twenty-five inches per annum, but the lowveld received only fifteen inches. West Nicholson was about 2000 feet. The climate and veld was totally different, making farming very different. The great difference in rainfall meant I could carry from twelve to fifteen cattle to the acre in Bulawayo whilst in West Nic I could carry only one beast per twenty-five acres.

There was also a noticeable difference in the veld. In the lowveld, mopani trees were predominant. They had an unusual feature in that their leaves in winter were highly nutritious; when they dropped in autumn the cattle grazed them under the trees and thus maintained quality and weight well into winter, whilst at Heany my cattle would be losing weight rapidly. This had financial implications because cattlemen were paid on a 'weight for grade' basis. Their weight was maintained whist the price increased every week.

I have told all this to give some background to a conversation I had with Uncle Bert. He had retired to Capetown and was on holiday in

Oswestry, staying with his sister, Aunty Em, who was the town Mayoress. Father had invited Uncle Bert to dinner, and since he had no transport my father asked me to pick him up and take him back after dinner. On the way back he asked me what I was doing. I explained I was working for Pip but had no real plans for the future.

He asked, "Why don't you come to Southern Rhodesia and make money growing tobacco?"

This sounded like a good idea, and Pip agreed with it, saying if he was not so incapacitated he would have gone to South Africa himself. In order to get into Southern Rhodesia you had to have a job, and Uncle Bert knew a tobacco farmer currently in England on holiday. I met him and he gave me a job. My father enabled me to qualify financially by lending me three hundred pounds, and I arrived in Bulawayo on 19 April 1949, exactly four years to the day I was commissioned at Sandhurst.

I left Southampton on the Union Castle liner, the 'Edinburgh Castle', a lovely high class luxury liner. There is little to report about the trip except for one story.

The ship was obviously full of South Africans, and one night they held a cultural evening in the lounge. I was fascinated. They dressed in national dress, the men in white shirts and embroidered waistcoats, the ladies in coloured dresses and 'kappies'. They sang; they danced; they read poetry and scriptures. They played the violin and accordions and did everything in Afrikaans, their national language. I yearned to belong to such a focused group and have recognised and admired their culture ever since. They have maintained it wherever they live. They stick together and are strong in their beliefs, especially their religion. The Dutch Reformed Church is a powerful influence in their lives. On board ship there used to be a competition to guess how many miles the ship had travelled the last twenty four hours, and the captain gave his estimate at about 10am (the competition closing at midday). After some days I spotted a method he was using. If his estimate was five hundred miles the actual would be one less. The next day it would be one more. The next day after that it would be two less, then two more. You bought as many tickets you could afford on your selected number and the total number of tickets bought for each estimate was constantly updated. If a lot of tickets were bought for one figure of mileage you avoided that number because there were too many people to share the total amount invested. I did well for a start, using my newfound secret until the captain changed his system. Today was to be three up so I put all my money on that number because that was the way the dice were falling, an absolute certainty. Unfortunately, the captain made his estimate suddenly ten up or down. I lost all my money of which I was very short anyway.

Uncle Bert very kindly met me in Capetown and took me for lunch in the 'Arthur's Seat Hotel' where he now lived with his wife. He put me on the train to Bulawayo and it was a couple of years before I saw him again in Rhodesia.

On the way to Bulawayo (two thousand miles away, a journey of two nights and three days) the countryside was dry and scrub-like and we didn't see any livestock or wildlife. Immigration people got on board at Plumtree, asked questions and looked at passports. My papers were all in order so I was in! An overriding memory is the sight of the major railway junction at De Aar and that one of the men who was sharing the compartment had smelly socks; we had to endure and live with this for the whole journey! We were certainly glad to arrive!

Last Days in England

Snakes Alive

7

Arrival

Southern Rhodesia

The next part of the story begins in Southern Rhodesia where I lived for the next sixty years. I went by train down to West Nicholson, a village in the lowveld, a journey of about eight hours on a very slow moving train, stopping at every little country station or siding. It was a long way – about one hundred and fifty miles – getting hotter by the hour. I stayed with Uncle Stan, Uncle Bert's younger brother, and with Aunty Tibb, Uncle Syd's widow. In no time I was on a tobacco farm, Umfurudzi Farm, in the highveld (the north of the country, also known as Mashonaland). The nearest town was Bindura, some eighteen miles away.

I lived in converted stables and had an African cookboy who did everything in the house: cooking, washing, ironing and cleaning. My priority was to learn the universal African language in southern Africa, called 'Chilapalapa' or 'Fanagalo', a language I used in Zambia, Mozambique and South Africa as well as in Rhodesia. I was proficient in it within three months. No African spoke English away from the towns so it was an imperative. There was a farm manager, a South African at first and then an Englishman who was a carpenter by trade but had left England to better himself, his wife and two young children; he became a fine farmer and made a fortune for the owner.

The farm covered three thousand acres and grew about seventy acres of Virginia tobacco a year as well as fifty acres of maize for staff consumption. Virginia tobacco cannot be grown in the same field more than twice because of nematode problems, hence the need for a lot of ground, new lands having to be stumped out every year. Virgin soil produced the best quality tobacco. Wood from the stumped land was used to cure the produce.

I learned there were three kinds of tobacco: Virginia, which we grew and what people would imagine tobacco to be; Burley, which was a tasteless filler; and Turkish, a highly flavoured variety.

Growing tobacco in Rhodesia

Virginia was flue cured; that means that after the leaves were picked they were put into a barn to cure. A barn was about twenty-five feet high and fifteen feet deep and wide. Inside were a series of racks to hold the tobacco leaves. The tobacco was brought in from the field, having been reaped leaf by leaf from the tobacco plant. A leaf from the middle of the plant could easily be three feet long.

Perhaps I should start at the beginning. Tobacco is first planted in seed beds which have to be sterilised by fire to kill root knot nematodes which inhibit plant growth. The seed is very, very small – almost like dust. It comes in a number of varieties which are bred by our Tobacco Research Station. When the seed beds are ready, after the burning ash had been removed and the soil surface cultivated by hand, the seed was sown by watering can with a rose, a seedbed being five feet wide. You went up one side with your watering can and down the other side stirring the can vigorously with a stick ensuring even distribution of the seed.

The beds were covered with hessian until germination and then gradually hardened off, exposing the plants to the sun and heat a little bit more each day. The seedlings would be ready for planting out in about six weeks. The field had to be prepared ready to receive the plants. Each planting station had to be marked out exactly to receive the individual plants. The plants were very carefully pulled out of the seed bed, covered with a wet sack and taken to the field. Next, a 'picannin' (a small boy) would drop each plant onto the planting station, and a man with a short handled 'badza' (hoe) would dig a hole with one hand and place the tender plant into it, firming the soil around it, usually with his feet. These workers never wore boots or shoes.

To keep the momentum going, plant after plant, was a tiring and skilful job. No time could be wasted as the day of planting had been selected as a propitious moment for the best take. Organisation and timing had to be in top order. Plant lengths would differ, and the planter had to dig his hole accordingly. We constantly had to implore them to make sure the longer plants were planted deep enough.

Tobacco is a weed with strong resistance to drought. It enjoyed sandy soils best because the soil nutrients could be controlled by correct fertilisation. Plants would grow five to six feet high and their leaves would be reaped by hand. Only ripe leaves were picked, a ripe leaf showing signs of going a beige colour. The reaper would take no more than three leaves per plant and put them under his arm. When he had enough leaves he would hand them over to a picannin who would place them in a hessian-lined crate called a 'madenga'. When a madenga was full it was placed on a trailer which, when reaping the field was complete, was taken by ox wagon to the barns.

Now another phase of preparation for curing took place. The madenga was placed in front of a worker called a 'tyer'. It was his job to tie the leaves, usually three at a time onto a stick called a 'mateppe' for it to be placed inside the barn. It was a skilful job, and it was always a joy to see these men doing it. A mateppe was placed on a 'y' stick at the front, and another one was placed at the other end to hold the mateppe level with the ground and at a suitable height for the tyer. Every mateppe had to be of equal length for stacking in the barn.

Each tyer had a picannin in front of him to hand him three leaves; the picannin had his back to the tyer and handed him the leaves behind his back, not looking at the tyer behind him. Co-operation between the two was vital for a continuous flow of production. Tyers would sing and have body movements almost like dancing to maintain a rhythm of operation. It is practically impossible to describe the atmosphere created to keep boredom at bay. It is natural for Africans to work like this, even in the most tedious of workplaces. The tyer tied one set of leaves on the left of the stick and the next one on the right. According to the size of the leaf the manager would instruct them how many 'hands' to tie on each mateppe. A 'hand' referred to the leaves handed to the tyer by the picannin.

When a mateppe was full, he would hand it to another labourer who would take it inside the barn and give it to a further labourer who would pass it up to the man stacking it in racks. Again the manager would instruct the stacker how many mateppes to put on a tier, this again being calculated by the density of the leaves which again was governed by the position on the plant where the leaves came from. The biggest leaves came from the middle of the plant. Barns would consist of lower, middle or top leaf.

Now to the curing. Virginia tobacco was flue cured as opposed to burley tobacco which was air cured. Outside the barn was a fire box which was fired by wood. The heat was led into the barn by flues (metal pipes) which went straight down the centre of the barn at floor level. When it reached the far end (the entrance to the barn) it divided left and right and went around the sides of the barn going back to where it started and exiting through a chimney. Heat was drastically controlled with a barn thermometer in each barn. This had a movable pointer, and the manager set the temperature at whatever was required for that stage of curing. Ventilators were built into the top of the barns as an aid to temperature control.

Workers worked day and night to control the heat in the barns by stoking the fire box with fresh wood as required. It normally took a week to cure a barn. The last important job was to dry the 'midrib', and this took considerable heat. In the process, the leaf became very, very dry and would shatter into powder at the slightest touch. Now the tobacco had to be removed, ready for the next batch of reaping, so steam was introduced into the barn (the leaves being very hygroscopic) and it became possible now to remove the mateppes without shattering the leaves which were now soft and pliable.

The steam came from a very large boiler designed for the job. There were sixteen barns on this farm, all piped up to carry steam. This was quite a large farm; you could calculate the size of a farm by the number of barns on it.

On being removed from the barn the tobacco was stacked until the curing season was over. Then it was categorised leaf by leaf into grades governed by colour (which varied considerably) and texture (how spotty the leaf was), purity in shape, tears and so on. Only experienced graders were used because it was by grades the tobacco was sold. It was then baled in 200lb bales and sent to the tobacco auction floor.

The floor in Salisbury was one of the biggest in the world. Buyers came from all over the world and bid for the tobacco, bale by bale. Each bale was opened up for the buyer to see and feel its quality. Once sold the bale was given a ticket naming the buyer and the price paid. If a farmer disagreed with the price he would tear the ticket and offer it again on another day. The auctioneer, a professional in the tobacco industry, walked down one side of the row of bales with the buyers on the other side. They knew the buyers and at the sale of each bale would call out the buyer's company name. To any visitor this was completely unintelligible as it was done in a sing-song voice at high speed. Going ahead of the auctioneer was an expert evaluator who would decide the price he thought was reasonable and would call out his estimate of the value per pound of that particular bale.

Tickets of the bales sold were immediately taken to an office, their total value calculated and the farmer given his cheque the same day. Of course, each grower's consignment was placed in its own line and sold as a continuous batch, making ticket collection easy. The tickets were taken to the office in a bunch; that would be the farmer's offering for the day.

An auctioneer's voice had to be trained to stand the strain of continuous use all morning. Every day the average price for the tobacco on offer was announced on the radio during the evening news as it was of such interest to the farming community.

The farmer I worked for was outstanding, and his average 'per pound' was way above the national average. He bought another farm at Mermaids Pool and sent me there to burn thirty thousand bricks so that he could build more barns. He was so successful he paid most of the farm off in one year because of the increased production caused by his larger barn capacity.

Moving on

I did not really enjoy tobacco farming and after eighteen months went to West Nicholson on holiday. There the Rogers' family offered me the position of Manager of their twenty thousand acre ranch, fifteen miles out of Bulawayo, at Heany Junction. The junction was a railway station where the railway line divided, one line going north to Salisbury and one south-east to West Nicholson, and the ranch straddled the railway. I gladly accepted and never doubted my ability to cope. Such arrogance! I was twenty-four years old at the time, going on twenty-five.

The ranch carried around twelve hundred head of Hereford beef stock, including twenty bulls and sixty trek oxen, one hundred and twenty dairy stock, ten breeding sows, two hundred and fifty acres under the plough and fifty acres of irrigation. It was divided into four paddocks, one of eight thousand acres and three of four thousand acres each. There were about thirty miles of fencing to be patrolled every day, ten miles of dirt roads to maintain, three dams, two windmills, three boreholes and two mine shafts for stock watering, gardening and domestic use.

There were around sixteen Africans as permanent staff who, with their families, gave me about sixty people to look after. They were unsophisticated and uneducated but, when you got to know them, were generally fine people.

Bulawayo is the capital of Matabeleland, a dry area and therefore not suitable for tobacco production nor other dryland crops; but since maize was the staple diet of the local people, over the years our Research Station developed drought-resistant strains of hybrid maize which produced satisfactory results when grown for workers. It was also grown for stock feed and not for sale commercially.

When I first went to Heany Junction Farm in 1950, the only working power we had was by trek oxen, big older animals used for motive power. I ploughed with a three furrow disc plough drawn by a span of sixteen oxen. You can imagine the skill required by the driver, the 'mchayili', when turning the plough at the headland so that it did not turn the plough over. The oxen were led by a picanin called a 'kokell' who had a ream attached to the horns of the leading yoke of oxen. The driver used a very long whip to control the oxen – at least twelve feet long – which he could crack with great effect around the ears of any lazy ox.

When the first settlers came into the country in the late 1800s they travelled from Northern Transvaal in trek wagons drawn by a span of sixteen oxen. The streets of Bulawayo were made wide enough to allow a span of sixteen oxen to turn their wagons. That equates today to about the width of fourteen cars side by side. There were large pavements either side of the road as well, wide enough for a car to drive along, although there were no cars in those days.

All transport on the farm was done by trek oxen using 'scotch carts' to carry milk to the station, take fencing materials to any part of the thirty miles or more of fencing to keep in repair, cattle feed for weaners, water where needed and so on. The advantage of trek oxen was that they never needed fuel, costly repairs or change of tyres and at the end of their usefulness could be sold at a profit! That was sound economics!

By living at the ranch, I was not as isolated from national life and events as I had been up north. Africans had a tribal society, and each local chief had much influence over the people. In the Heany area, Chief Kayisa Ndweni became a good friend, and I learned much of the national history from him. He spoke excellent English and was much respected nationally.

Africans had a poor reputation amongst Europeans, being uneducated and unsophisticated to a degree. I believe that some time before I arrived in the country they were not allowed to walk on the pavement in the towns. There was a war fought against Europeans early in the nineties with many European farmers being butchered to death. This was enough for the Africans to be called savages by the Europeans, who denied them much social improvement. They were strongly tribal, having little regard, if any, for the Shonas in Mashonaland.

The tribal system with hereditary Chiefs and elected Headmen (tribal elders) worked well; if it were at all possible the answer to African government would have been a benevolent dictatorship – but European prosperity became the African's dream. When Europeans introduced a 'one man one vote' system, Africans were not used to making decisions for themselves, preferring to follow what the Chief said. After all, his family had been ruling them for generations, and they trusted that he knew best.

When working with them, if an African was given a choice how to do something on the farm, he would refuse to make it, saying, "You are my father; you tell me what to do." Because I was the manager I had a supreme position on the farm, and even though I was only twenty five, they wanted me to tell them what to do, not to ask them to make a decision. This created a dictatorial attitude in me because the decision-making was expected and the ranch could not run without it.

Every farm had a 'bossboy' who was held in supreme honour amongst the workers. The key was to tell him what you wanted and he would relay it to the workers and get it done. In that way you maintained his reputation as their representative. I had much respect for the bossboy I inherited as he had worked under at least four European managers yet never adopted a superior attitude even though he was twice my age and knew that I knew nothing about ranching in Matabeleland.

Strangely enough, one of the managers who had been there just before the war was a cousin of my cousin Peter Humphries. His name was Tim Humphries and he lived a few miles from Old Marton. My bossboy remembered him well and spoke well of him.

I lived on my own with a good cook to do all the work that a wife would normally do. Not having a wife was a distinct drawback, but the conditions were so hard that I was afraid to get married in case I married just for the sake of marrying.

The danger of being alone came home to me one weekend. I was working in my office, a 'rondavel', one Saturday afternoon when most workers were off duty and attending beer drinks – an important social activity every weekend – so there was no-one around (not that I expected anyone to be). There I was, sitting at my desk at about 3pm, when I noticed something moving in the doorway. I recognised it instantly as a cobra when it hooded and struck at my leg, which was bare. My brain must have worked without my knowledge for I had shifted my leg and the snake missed, catching the edge of my boot. It was angry but did not strike again. I was terrified because it was under the door, showing about three feet of itself and covering my escape. I leapt onto my chair, hoping it would hold my weight, scared the snake would attack again. The only possible weapon available to me was a metal cash box full of coins I had on the desk. So, hoping for the best, I threw it down on the snake and, wonder of wonders, killed it.

When I tried to pull the dead snake from under the door, I found out why it had not attacked me by coming after me. It had a huge bulge in its stomach, having killed and eaten a rat, which prevented it from entering the room and attacking me further. A cobra doesn't normally miss when it strikes, and had it not been for the rat it would have bitten me with fatal consequences. Although Bulawayo Hospital was just fifteen miles away, a cobra's venom is so toxic I would have been dead before I got there. I would have died a lonely death since there was not a worker to be seen; even if I had been married, a wife would not have reached me in time.

On another occasion when I was on my own, I was charged and knocked down by a wild ox when trying to load it into a railway truck to send it to Bulawayo for slaughter. We had loaded ninety-nine out of the hundred I had in the railway loading kraal. This last one was a 'Binya' (meaning he was a 'mad' animal). He had escaped my effort to load him the previous year, and we had been unable to catch him before he literally jumped two fences and returned to his home paddock.

No matter how hard we tried he would not be loaded. I had two or three herdsmen in the holding kraal but they could not persuade nor drive him into the railway truck. I was standing outside the kraal fence and realised I should set an example to the workers. Grabbing a herdsman's 'knobkerrie' I entered the kraal and chased him myself. He refused to cooperate, and I made the mistake of getting too close to him. He leaped at me, hitting me straight in the chest. I was flattened. He knelt down beside me and attempted to gore me with his head, but fortunately, he was de-horned. I cried out to the bossboy to hit him, which would not have done any good even if he could have done so. I managed to roll out of the kraal, and then the ox went and loaded himself into the railway truck, much to our amazement. Fortunately, the men holding the other oxen in the truck saw him coming and opened the door at exactly the right time to let him in and keep the others from escaping. It was all done in a flash.

I needed a wife that day but didn't have one. I took myself off to the doctor the next day and discovered I had six cracked ribs. With no shoulder to cry on I had to get on with managing the ranch all strapped up with goodness-knows-what.

Another dangerous thing happened about that time. I was walking through our breeding herd in a kraal having just dipped about 350 cows. I had an African herdsman beside me, and we were just checking to make sure we had dealt with any problems – ear ticks, snares around legs, cuts and any other damages – when two cows beside us began to fight. The losing cow swung around 180 degrees and, before the herdsman could get

Snakes Alive

out of the way, her horn opened up his cheek so that I could see his teeth and tongue. I had to rush him to the Bulawayo Mpilo Hospital some seventeen miles away to get him stitched up. In Sindebele, Mpilo means 'life', a good name for a hospital.

A few weeks later I had another lucky snake escape. My boss, Uncle Stan Rogers, and I were watching our breeding stock, about 350 cows, leaving the dipping kraal after being dipped. Dipping was a legal necessity to prevent the spread of gallsickness, redwater and blackwater fever, ear ticks and a host of other minor diseases. We were watching them leave the kraal when I was aware of movement in front of me. I looked down and saw a huge cobra at my feet. It moved away to the left but curled back again and moved to the right. It could not get away because I was inadvertently standing on its tail! My bare legs were an invitation to disaster! (I always wore my socks rolled down to my boots because we had a grass called 'spear grass' which, as its name implies, had seeds like spears or needles; to get them in your socks was agony). Uncle Stan always wore long trousers so was not at as much risk. I nudged him and showed him the snake. He quietly handed me his walking stick, and when I took my foot off its tail it shot off but I was ready for it and killed it. It must have been seven feet long, a monster in that day and a lucky escape (but I still kept my socks rolled down!)

Another effect of spear grass in Rhodesia meant you could not carry sheep with wool – for obvious reasons. We had to crossbreed the Black Head Persian breed (which had hair and not wool) with the European exotic breeds like Dorset or Wiltshire Horn in order to put meat on them. The Persians had little meat and stored their fat in their tails. They were called fat-tailed sheep as a consequence.

A couple of other near misses come to mind. The house had no toilet inside but had one (called a long-drop) at the bottom of the garden. In it I kept a twenty litre tin of disinfectant called Kerol. When visiting the toilet one day I was sitting there when I noticed a snake coiled up between the tin and the wall. It was so close I could touch it. What an aid to urgent bowel movement! It was either a green mamba or a boomslang (I could never tell the difference, both being bright green and most deadly). I dashed out quickly enough, snakes having a strange habit of leaving you alone if you didn't disturb them.)

Arrival

On another occasion I went to a local church service in the nearby army camp where a minister from Bulawayo came on a Sunday. Walking up to kneel on a cushion to receive communion and just as the minister moved to serve the next person, a cobra came and curled itself around the cushion I was about to kneel on. I said nothing to anyone and stayed kneeling until everyone had been served. This was to protect any lady wearing a skirt, and having bare legs, from being bitten, since she would have no protection from the fangs of the snake. I had the protection of trousers which could soak up venom and also prevent the fangs from reaching my leg. I watched that cushion to the end of the sermon, never hearing a word the minister said. At the end of the service I went to the back of the chapel, found a shovel and killed the snake, which was about four feet long.

The only time I ever saw a python was when I was driving to Bulawayo and I hit what looked like a stick lying across the road. It was not a stick but a python, but I recognised it too late to stop. The truck went bump, bump over it. I turned round to see it, but it had returned to the bush so I never saw it again. It must have been a big brute because the road was twenty two feet wide and its head was over the centre of the road with its tail still in the bush on the side of the road. It would have been fifteen feet long at least. Fortunately it had not taken offence at me. Pythons have a blunt hard head and nose which they use as a weapon to stun a victim so that they cannot run away (pythons are very slow movers so they cannot quickly pursue a victim). In this case it could easily have stunned me if it was waiting for revenge.

One amusing incident occurred regarding a python. A worker came to me to say he had seen a python in the calf paddock. He could only see a portion of it in the long grass but had marked the spot by tying grass heads together. I was milking at the time, and as soon as I finished I rushed to the house to get my twelve bore shot gun. It was evening and the light was fading. The worker took me to the spot, and the snake was still there. I could not see which way it was facing and crept up to it as close as I dared. I was afraid of getting too close as my only view of it was its middle section and I did not know how close its head was – a dangerous position to be in since it was possible for it to swing round and attack if I had misjudged its length. In the twilight I was only a few feet away.

I had to do something quickly before it got dark. So warning the African with me I fired at the reptile, fully expecting an attack. I had a spare cartridge in my gun and was geared up to fire a second time. Imagine my surprise when the 'snake' leapt up rigidly in the air, showing itself to be a stick and not a python. The stick was beautifully mottled just like a python, and even the African had been fooled. He had seen it in daylight so I could be excused for thinking it was a python. I took the stick home and playfully threw it at an African who nearly died of fright!

A railway line cut the ranch into three sections, the first a four thousand acre paddock, the next an eight thousand acre paddock leaving two four thousand acre paddocks. The line came from Bulawayo, and a branch went down to West Nicholson in the lowveld whilst the main line continued on to Salisbury.

The eight thousand acre paddock was a beautiful place, a vast savannah veld with very few trees. You could see for miles with no obstructions in view. It was lovely to see Secretary Birds stalking through the veld looking for snakes. When they found one they would pick it up in their feet and fly high then drop it to the ground. There they would finish it off and eat it.

Bird life was prolific, very colourful and, to a degree, noisy with song. It was always a treat to see Kori Bustards ranging through the tall grass, some of it six feet high, looking for rats and lizards and snakes too. Strangely there was very little game, probably because there was so little tree cover.

An impressive bird in the veld was the wild turkey, also called a ground hornbill. It was a large bird as big, if not bigger, than a domestic turkey with a deep, booming, echoing, rolling 'boom' of a voice echoing across the veld. They also ranged through the veld in pairs as though they were kings of their domain.

Away from the open veld there were numerous, beautiful birds, my favourite being the Crested or Crowned Crane. It was an unforgettable experience to see them flying overhead on the way to the nearby dam, calling to each other, "mahem, mahem" in clear voices. Africans called them Mahem because of their distinctive call which seemed to come out of the heavens above as they flew by.

Other birds were exquisite in plumage and song – the Red Breasted Shrikes being so distinctive, the Hueglin's Robin being one of the finest songsters in Africa. It was also called the White-browed Robin and had an unusual way of calling. When first you heard it you thought it was a hundred yards away but its song came closer and closer until you realised it was in the tree above you. It was wonderful to be woken up in the morning to such exquisite music.

Some other birds with distinctive voices were the barbet family and the louries. There were two varieties of barbets. The first was the Speckled Barbet which would sit on a branch and 'trill' continuously for several minutes non-stop. Its relative, the Black Headed Barbet, was a really different bird caller from any other I ever heard. At first you thought it was one bird but in fact it was two. I don't think it ever called by itself. The male would call 'two' followed by the female calling 'puddly'. That is how the ornithologists describe it in their bird books, but it is a bit more like "whoo puddly" without any gap between the calls. So you had "two-puddly, two-puddly, two-puddly" four or five times. If the male called "two" without a reply he would stop and wait, then start again

The Grey Lourie was another distinctive caller. He was known as the 'go-away' bird because his call sounded just like that. Prince Philip once said he had heard about a "Bare-faced Go-away" bird but I cannot remember the country he was visiting at the time.

A beautiful bird was the Paradise Fly Catcher with its lovely long russett tail; when it sang in the tree above you, you had to stop and listen.

Hornbills were plentiful and could be identified by their distinctive up and down flight as well as their honking call. Redwinged Starlings were very obvious by their red wings; their brothers, the Common Starling, had the most gorgeous, iridescent plumage which altered every time the sun shone in a different way on their bodies. Doves, and to a lesser extent pigeons, were constant companions and hardly a moment of the day went by without one sitting cooing on your roof.

Finches were common birds, Red Fire Finches being a favourite, together with Blue Finches. They were tiny little birds, smaller than wrens, and were always found in flocks on the ground looking for ants and seeds. Lovely little things!

Weaver birds were most interesting in the construction of their amazing nests. Red Bishop birds were bad tempered creatures but beautiful to see (bad tempered in that they noisily and actively defended their territory). They also built hanging nests, particularly amongst reed beds.

Pied crows were aggressive birds and tended to drive away smaller species. On the dams, ducks and teal were found in abundance and at Heany Junction were often the target of the guns of my friends and I.

Swallows and swifts were visitors in summer and never built nests, preferring to breed in Europe. It was an amazing sight to see them catching flying ants of the smaller variety as the ants came out of their breeding nests in the ground. You could hear the snap of their beaks as they caught each one. Birds that we shot for the pot were guinea fowl and francolin, rather like a partridge but known locally as a pheasant. We had egrets close to water, and white storks were late summer visitors from North Africa.

One day as I was driving into Bulawayo past the Khumalo Airport at the entrance to the city, I saw what I thought looked like a white UFO flying across the airfield. It circled around the airfield, white and flat like a saucer, for hundreds of yards. I had to stop and watch it, believing I was seeing something unique and genuine – a flying saucer over Bulawayo!! The saucer suddenly turned and I saw it was a flight of white Egrets flying in a perfect formation. There were probably fifty birds in the group. It is almost impossible to describe on paper, so perfect was their formation. At one time I was only about a hundred yards away and had a very clear view. I can understand why some people are convinced they have seen a UFO.

Living in England now, I miss the constant companionship and songs of the birds. What a pleasure to have tea on your lawn to the accompaniment of doves a few yards away, Hueglin Robins in the trees and crows with their unwelcome, raucous cawing nearby. Such recollections!

It was rumoured that a family of elephants had gone through the ranch many years ago but I met no-one who had actually seen them. If it was true they would have devastated the fencing. Cattle had an uncanny way of finding a break in fences. The grass on the other side of the hill was always greener, and since ranches were big they could wander a long way before being found. All our stock, including dairy stock, were branded on the left flank with our registered brand. That was an infallible proof of ownership.

The eight thousand acre paddock had lovely views; you could stand at the gate and look around for miles without seeing any housing or human life, only your own stock, sometimes the odd buck but nothing else. Absolute bliss to me!

Veld fires were a menace and dangerous. This paddock was burnt out completely one Sunday afternoon when there was a high wind and the grass was bone dry. The grass had not had rain for six months, a natural phenomenon in Rhodesia where it rained for just five months of the year. Fortunately I had moved the breeding stock to better grazing, some four hundred head, so no damage was done to my grazing programme.

The railway station was also the post office, and I went regularly there to pick up the post. One day I had an altercation with an African and was giving him a piece of my mind in flowery language. Then I heard a voice behind me say, "Your brother Tom wouldn't like to hear you talk like that." Surprise, surprise! It transpired that the owner of the voice had served in the Air Force in the war, had been de-mobbed and had become a Ferguson tractor salesman, selling a 'Fergie' to my father. He had decided to return to the Air Force and had told my father he was going to Rhodesia. Father had said, "My son Ted is there; look him up," and in spite of the vagueness of the information he was now talking to me. There was an air force base next to the ranch, and since I was well known there he had found me. I met another air force officer named John Phillips who came from a village close to Tom's farm; I believe it was Knockin. It's a small world!

The ranch had been rich in gold and there were five old gold workings there, all of them shallow surface type veins. Some of the old workings became flooded with water, and I used them for gardening and stock watering and to supply water for workers who lived nearby. Driving past the ranch some weeks after I had left I noticed a three stamp mill near the Bulawayo road. Someone had found gold 'under my nose', as it were, because I had never found any. However, the mine lived up to the local history, and it closed down within a couple of years.

Altogether I was responsible for the welfare of about fifty to sixty African workers, their wives and children. Their weekend entertainment was drinking 'kaffir beer' which they brewed with written permission from me, the Ranch Manager. This made it legal and they held drinking parties every weekend. They sold the beer to make extra money for themselves. I issued only one licence a week.

There were frequent fights over women, and I often spent Sundays taking casualties to hospital in Bulawayo. At a party near my house an African died and the police were called. The post mortem found he had drowned in his own vomit. Another time an African came to my house one Sunday afternoon wearing a blood-soaked raincoat. He had been hit on the head with an axe – a homemade tool, made out of car spring steel and less than two inches wide but sharpened to a fine edge. These homemade axes were vicious weapons, usually used for chopping wood. On this occasion this chap had had a fight with someone who had hit him on the head with his axe – a 'demu', they called it. Blood poured down his raincoat and he was soaked in it. It was so bad that I refused to let him sit inside my truck and made him sit in the back as I drove him to hospital. Such was the wound that I could see his blood pulsing in his head. I waited until he was stitched up, then drove him back to his kraal and then reported it to the police. That was normal weekend behaviour: drinking, fighting, stealing, arguing and so on.

Witchdoctors were a problem. Even the biggest African was terrified of them. Their influence was everywhere. Witchdoctors included women, Mbuya Nehanda being the most notorious. (After independence, the main hospital in Harare was re-named after her.) I had one case fifty yards from my house. A female witchdoctor threatened a worker, a fine young twenty-three-year-old man, who was found hanged in his hut the next day.

Africans were adamant that chameleons were possessed by evil spirits and were terrified of them. Even Government officials, supposedly well educated, were convinced it was possible to get on the back of a hyena and it would fly you from Bulawayo to Harare during the night. I heard a minister say this on television. Another Government Minister, when visiting a drought-stricken area which was short of water, advised

Arrival

the local Chief and Headmen to consult the local witchdoctor to tell them where to dig for water. At times this was not difficult because wild fig trees grew above water. Indeed, on one of my properties a well had been dug next to a fig tree. There was water there at one time, but it was now dry.

They were strong believers in river gods. They claimed that anyone under the influence of a river god could lie on the bottom of a river and come out alive after days there. The old ways still had a strong influence on the people.

One of my favourite activities was bird shooting, especially duck, pheasant and guinea fowl. On Saturday afternoons I would invite some officers from the nearby Air Force base to come shooting, one of the most enthusiastic being the Base Commander, Group Captain Freddie Rump.

One weekend I had four guest shooters including Freddie Rump. Not having any luck on my ranch, with permission I took them to a neighbouring farm. I was using my farm truck which had low sides, about knee high. Three were in the back of the truck leaning on the cabin whilst I had one in the cab with me, a doctor. Driving up a road a pheasant ran across it just in front of the truck and into the bush. I swung the truck around to the right to face the bird so that the guns on the back could get a shot. Unfortunately, I swung the truck too quickly and all three of them fell on top of one another. Freddie fell on the stock of his gun and broke it. Someone fell on Freddie and knocked him unconscious, but thankfully no gun went off. I was shouting, "Shoot! Shoot!" before I realised what had happened. The doctor, a Squadron Leader, leaped out only to find Freddie looking dead, but he soon came round with broken ribs for his trouble. That night was to be Freddie's farewell party with the Mayor of Bulawayo attending. Freddie had been appointed Air Attache in the British Embassy in Pretoria. He was too sick to attend so his farewell went off like a damp squib with me getting the blame. I was a member of their Officers' Mess so attended automatically and guiltily, a rather difficult end to Freddie's tour of duty. He was a very fine man, and we had had many successful shooting parties. An unfortunate send-off after a wonderful tour of duty; he was a fine shot to boot. One story he told was when he visited the game park Wankie and was charged by an elephant but managed to escape in his car.

Having run the ranch for more than two years without a single break, day or night, I was invited to go fishing one weekend to the Shangaani river a couple of hundred miles away, on the way to Victoria Falls. Since there was very little farm activity of much importance, I accepted and left one Friday afternoon to return on Sunday.

Someone had to lend me a rod, and we had quite a successful haul of fish, particularly bream, a very edible fish. I caught a Bottlenose Fish, which had an unusual protection device: if you held it by its nose and tail you got a considerably powerful electric shock, especially if you were standing in water. I was suitably punished for having the temerity of removing it from its environment!

Having had an enjoyable break from being on duty 24/7 (as is the modern expression) and arriving home with two days' unshaven face and smelling somewhat of fish, I came back to find one of my bosses, Jack Rogers, had come down from West Nicholson to spend the weekend on the ranch. Of course, he had found the ranch without a manager. I was horrified and chagrined to be caught red-handed neglecting my responsibilities. He challenged me and asked me if I did this frequently. I answered that I had been a loyal servant to the Rogers for more than two years without a day off and was ashamed to be found out the only time I had neglected my duties.

Strangely enough I never heard a further word of my offence and must conclude Jack never reported me to the rest of the family. Certainly, my immediate boss, Uncle Stan, never mentioned it. He was never afraid to question me on some of my management decisions.

My pigs were not doing too well financially so I decided to deal with another company whose pig food I thought would give me better results. However, we did not have an account with them and I couldn't buy from them openly so I devised a way of purchasing their pig food. I sold a lot of empty sacks to the company I usually bought my pig food from and asked them to give me a cheque in my name so that, unknown to them, I could pay cash to the other company. This they did but reported me, in writing, to the Rogers. Uncle Stan challenged me on this but I was able to show him the receipt for what I had paid for and not the company.

Arrival

Before I left the tobacco farm I was sent, with a senior African, to investigate the possibility of recruiting labour from northern Matabeleland where jobs were hard to get. We crossed into Northern Rhodesia via the Victoria Falls Bridge over the Zambezi river and motored eighty miles up the river, arriving opposite the Kazanguls Fishing camp on the Rhodesian side and just close to the Caprivi Strip. It was eight o'clock at night, and as we crossed in a small boat with an outboard motor, a hippopotamus surfaced almost under the boat, no more than six feet from the side of the boat. Fortunately, it was just beyond the side of the boat and not beneath us; otherwise we would have been tipped into the river.

I caught my only tiger fish on this trip although I was not there to go fishing. International competitions were held annually by teams from all over the world, especially from South Africa, for the most fish, the heaviest fish and so on. Tiger fish had the most vicious teeth and would deeply scar a metal fishing spoon. On the day I caught one we were fishing near the Caprivi Strip and came across a family of hippos about seventy yards away. They expressed a dangerous interest in us. One of the people in the boat had a rifle and put a shot between the leading hippos. They reacted violently and the leading two leapt out of the water in a violent charge with their enormous mouths gaping and ready to eat us all, which they were quite capable of doing. With only a few yards to spare, our outboard motor started first time and we escaped. Hippos are responsible for more human deaths in Africa than any other animal.

Snakes Alive

Arrival

"The cobra" by Sue Hazeldine, Living Waters Church

Snakes Alive

8

Marriage and Metabeleland

Modern Progress

Early in 1953 the political structure of the country began to change. Roy Welensky, a train driver in Northern Rhodesia (a trade union activist, I believe), had a vision of federating Northern Rhodesia, Southern Rhodesia and Nyasaland into one economic union. This came about as he dreamed.

Sir Godfrey Huggins was Prime Minister of Southern Rhodesia whilst the other two countries were British Protectorates. Economic resources were pooled and much benefit accrued to the participants. So we changed our name to the Federation of Rhodesia and Nyasaland. Later, this collapsed and we changed our name simply to Rhodesia under Sir Edgar Whitehead. In about 1962 a referendum was held to advance African participation in government and business. This was passed by a two thirds majority. The Nationalist leader at that time was Joshua Nkomo, a Methodist lay preacher and leader of the Matabele people. He was an able speaker of nationalist rhetoric and had a large following in Matabeleland where he was idolised. He had little following in Mashonaland, but he had the following of the media and his voice was heard across the country. He rejected the referendum and demanded immediate independence. This caused a backlash among the electorate, predominantly European, which then formed the Rhodesia Front party under Winston Field who came to power as Prime Minister.

After many years of RF rule the country changed its name to Zimbabwe Rhodesia under Bishop Abel Muzorewa, a popular African choice. He governed with Ian Smith until independence from the British Government was obtained in 1980 and Robert Mugabe came to power.

There was instant reaction from the Matabele because Mugabe was a Shona and the Matabele knew they would be outnumbered in any national vote. They tried to break away and did all sorts of strange things to make their power felt. There was an undeclared war between them, and Mugabe imported North Koreans to train his army in dealing with dissidents. The Matabele were hammered and thousands were killed, I believe. Their bodies were dumped into disused mine shafts which could hold hundreds of bodies.

Joshua Nkomo fled the country dressed as a woman – so the media reported – and one cartoon humorously depicted him fleeing across the Umzingwane river dressed in a frilly dress, the humour being that Nkomo was a large, fat man. He went to London and was kept by Tiny Rowlands in a posh hotel. Eventually Rowlands got tired of the cost and moved him to cheaper accommodation. He came back to Zimbabwe and landed up as Deputy President, a political appointment to appease the Matabele. I considered him a brainless individual, but he had some good sons. One of them came to me when I was a manager in the AFC and tried to buy a farm through us – no political motives involved.

He could not fulfil all our financial conditions so he asked me to hold the farm for a week and not let anyone else buy it. He came back a week later with the extra money having, as he said, been to the Middle East – Saudi Arabia I believe.

The country's name was once more changed to Zimbabwe which will probably be for good. The troubles that the country has gone through, and is still going through, must be laid at the feet of Joshua Nkomo for his rejection of the referendum. He mis-read the situation which was for change to bring Africans into the mainstream of society from which they had been excluded. He died a few years ago.

The chaos which ensued was tragic and could have been avoided had the referendum been accepted. Harold Macmillan didn't help with his "wind of change" speech. The chaos is still there today. Ian Smith's assertion that "never in a thousand years" would Africans rule themselves is being proved right in that they rule not by consent but by power. They cannot overcome their avarice and yearning for absolute dictatorial power. Once in power they lose control of human rights in order to stay there. Go and ask Mugabe. He will give up control only 'over his dead body'. Many years ago I heard a leading African academic, a man without political bias and during the beginning of independence when hopes were high, saying an African leader like Mugabe would destroy a country before giving up power. I did not believe him then, thinking democracy would prevail, but I underestimated the unrestrained wickedness of Mugabe and his ilk. Ian Smith and that academic knew them better than I did!

So much for that bit of history!

In 1953, my twin sister, Ann, wrote to me and said she wanted to get married, asking whether I would be her best man. I had worked for the Rogers for three years without taking any official time off so they gave me three months' leave to go to England for this purpose.

The boss boy was excellent and could cope for three months during that time of the year – a quiet time without hassles of ploughing, planting, cultivating, hoeing and so on, with Uncle Stan frequently coming down from West Nicholson where he lived, some hundred and fifty miles from the ranch. So I said yes, I would come. I couldn't travel by sea because it would take too much of my holiday time; I had to fly. So I decided that if I was going to fly, never having done so before, I would do it in style by flying in the Comet, recently put into service by BOAC.

It was the first commercial jet airliner to fly to Johannesburg and back so this would be a great occasion indeed, to fly in such a prestigious aircraft. It was expensive but I was given three months' salary in advance, sold my motorbike and landed in England with £125 for my three months' holiday. This was not a lot if I wanted to buy anything or get around. I wanted a car but it was beyond me.

I flew to England a day or two after the Queen's coronation. A week before I flew, Hillary and Tensing had conquered Everest and the Queen had been crowned. Now I was going to England after four years out of the country. I would be somewhat lonely, coming from an unknown environment to all at Old Marton. So Ann said she would ask her chief bridesmaid to stay on for a day or so after the wedding to keep me company.

This was an Irish lady that she worked with in physical education in a large girls' school in Liverpool; she had often visited Old Marton on school holidays. Ann said she was pretty, Irish and intelligent. We met a few days before the wedding and Ann's ploy worked: she is now my wife! I used my meagre holiday money to visit her in Ireland and to buy an engagement ring. I arrived back in Bulawayo with £5 in my pocket and no one to meet me as arrangements got fouled up. I had to use my money to hire a taxi to take me the fifteen miles to the ranch.

In those days, when you crossed the equator flying south, you were given a certificate with the aircraft number on it and the date in commemoration of your journey with BOAC. This was called "crossing the line". The aeroplane I returned in went on to Jo'burg, returned to London and then flew to Bombay. It fuelled up in Rome on the return journey, took off and blew up over the Mediterranean. I was lucky it didn't happen earlier when I was in it.

When flying to England we landed at Entebbe airport in Uganda at midnight. We disembarked, and as I was leaving the plane I stepped outside and immediately stepped back again because the heat was so intense. It was so hot that I thought the jet engines were still running. Like smaller airports today, you got off the plane by steps and went to the building by bus.

On the way back we stopped off there again and our departure was delayed because of thunderous weather in the district. When we did start off down the runway the ends of the wings bounced up and down until I thought they would fall off and wondered when would we come to the end of the runway and take off. The wings were still flapping up and down, and I thought the runway needed re-surfacing or something, so many were the potholes. I glanced at my watch and discovered we had been airborne thirty minutes. Fear seems to have been the problem!

Margaret came out to Rhodesia the next year; we were married at West Nicholson on 19th April 1954 and are still together fifty-six years later. We had no blood relatives at the wedding, only about twelve people there. There was no bridesmaid or best man. The church we were married in was a community church dedicated to St. Nicholas. Whoever he was I don't know, and we were the first to be married there.

The Bulawayo Chronicle had a field day of mistakes when reporting the occasion. If I remember correctly it reported that Mr & Mrs Nicholson were married at St. Nicholson's church at West Nicholas! Sounds a bit far-fetched, but I think that was what was reported. So I was commissioned at Sandhurst on 19th April 1945, arrived in Southern Rhodesia on 19th April 1949 and was married on 19 April 1954 – a most propitious date indeed!

In September of that year we moved to another thirteen thousand acre farm, Springvale, to manage a pedigree herd of Jersey dairy cows and perhaps eight hundred head of motley beef stock.

There was a polio epidemic raging around the country at that time, and we were advised to stay away from crowds etc. to avoid infection. We never went to cinemas etc., so it was no hassle to us to stay at home. However, despite our precautions I was diagnosed with polio on 30th January 1955. I was put into the Bulawayo Isolation Hospital immediately. Margaret was heavily pregnant and had to be isolated in the Bulawayo Cecil Hotel. The baby came a week later, and she had to phone for a taxi to take her to the hospital. So our first child, Terry, was born on 8th February 1955 whilst I was in hospital. I was not allowed to write to her because it was claimed the paper could carry the polio germs. Our doctor would visit Margaret and collect a letter from her and deliver it to me.

I had the non-paralytic kind of polio and had to be isolated for three weeks. After a few days I said to the doctor that I felt really well and was, in my opinion, definitely over the worst. His reply was that I was still a very sick man and that I should avoid all unnecessary movement as this could bring on paralysis. I hated bedpans so tried to go to the toilet when the sister was not looking, really not believing what the doctor had said – or at least willing to take a risk because I felt so well. This was, of course, comparative because I had felt so terribly ill before and my feeling better was only in relation to the bad feeling I had had at first.

There was a difference of opinion amongst the medical fraternity as to the quarantine period necessary to avoid infection. The city or Urban Medical Officer said it was three weeks so I was duly discharged from the Isolation Hospital after a three week stay there.

Margaret was now back in the Cecil Hotel; we went there after she came to take me out of hospital and introduce me to our almost two-week-old son, Terry. The Rural Medical Officer of Health said the quarantine period was four weeks so I could not return to the farm for a further week!

Whilst in hospital, a farmer friend was brought in having had a nightmare experience on the way. That year, and at that very time, the rains had been unusually heavy. On our farm we recorded forty-four inches instead of the normal twenty-five. Because the roads became impassable to vehicular traffic he had to be brought to hospital by ox wagon. There were no tarmac roads then. On the way in, he was stranded between two impassable rivers. He negotiated one river successfully but before he got to the next river, some ten miles further on, it rained heavily again so the river behind him came down in flood again as did the one in front of him. He was stranded with a roaring temperature for twenty-four hours and eventually arrived at the hospital after a three day journey which should have taken one day, that is, by ox wagon. He had spent two nights in the wagon without medical attention. He was paralysed from the neck down and his wife was not allowed to enter his single ward since his infection was so virulent. She had to sit on a chair on the verandah outside and try to talk to him through a door from there. When I had been in England the previous year, my mother had given me an electric razor so I used to go into his ward and shave him every morning. This went on for a week and then he died. What an appalling experience for his wife.

9

Farming

We were now allowed to go back to the farm and pick up our lives again but this time with a baby. All went well to begin with, but Terry started to show signs of sickness after a year or so, which meant many trips to see doctors.

One day when he was nearly two years old I took him down to see some puppies one of my dogs had had. Whilst looking at them in the bush a hornet stung Terry on the back of his neck, and I rushed to the house some fifty yards away. Carrying him over my shoulder he vomited down my back. It was obvious he was in trouble.

I changed my shirt and put Joy, then about nine months old, into her pram on the back seat of the car. We took off at high speed for Bulawayo, travelling on a dirt road. I went around a corner so fast that the car skidded, bucked and jumped – so wildly that Joy was thrown out of the pram, falling screaming onto the floor of the car. I had to stop to pick her up but didn't have time to console her, just dumped her crying, back into her pram. Getting back into the car I looked at Terry and couldn't recognise him for he was completely and obscenely bloated beyond recognition. Margaret thought he was dead.

We had to travel about four miles through a native reserve where you could expect cattle, donkeys, dogs and chickens at any turn. Fortunately we encountered nothing. We hit the Bulawayo road, turned right and headed out for the city at top speed, ignoring all speed limits over the ten mile journey. We arrived at the doctor's house but he was not there. We sped off to the Bulawayo General Hospital's outpatients department and took Terry in, carrying Joy at the same time. We had been there only a few minutes when our own doctor walked in. What a relief. How he got there so quickly I never found out. He gave Terry an injection of adrenalin directly into his heart and he recovered. Two hours later we were back on the farm with Terry playing on the lounge carpet as if nothing had happened. However, he died a few months later of what then was called 'fibrocystic disease of the pancreas'. It was a terrible blow.

Around that time we had an infestation of snakes. We killed fourteen cobras in the house and garden in one month. They were everywhere. One day Margaret heard a knocking noise in the bedroom and saw a frog trying to escape from a cobra, leaping under a wardrobe trying to escape from a snake. The cobra went into an empty suitcase, and I had to carry it outside with a loaded shotgun in my hand ready for action. Outside I opened it and shot the snake when it came out.

Another time she put the baby in its pram under a shady awning for fresh air and its sleep. Later, when the baby woke up, she wheeled the pram to the back door and took the child out. She took him to a bedroom and went back to the pram to collect his toys. In the pram where the baby had been was a cobra.

I was working at my desk at one end of the large kitchen with Joy playing behind my chair. I turned round to speak to her and found a cobra where she had been seconds before. She was still crawling, was nippy and fast and was adept at catching frogs or anything else that dared to move when she was around. If she had seen the snake she would have grabbed it and been killed.

One breakfast time Margaret said to look behind me, and there was a snake climbing up the mosquito netting door trying to get in from the verandah.

Walking down a road near the house, a snake shot across it, six feet in front of me. Snakes move in a letter S formation, but this chap was like a straight rod and 'thrummed' as it passed, obviously an escape mechanism. A few days later and in the same area, I was walking behind a tractor cutting lucerne with a mid-mounted mower when the same thing happened; a snake as straight as a rod shot between me and the tractor. It practically touched my leg, but I couldn't hear anything because of the tractor engine. In all the articles I have read on snakes I have never read of this behaviour.

Some years later on another farm, at ten o'clock at night, Margaret went to see one of our children who was sleeping in another room and, fortunately, took her torch with her. As she opened the door to the bedroom she shone her torch down and found she was straddling a cobra on the doorstep. It slithered under a bed and into a box. By the torch light I could see the snake's head in the box. We had a small house with a low tin roof so I was reluctant to use my shotgun because of the noise it would make. I knew my neighbour had a .22 rifle which would not make so much noise as to frighten the children, and I had no intention of arguing with a snake in the half dark armed only with a brush or a stick. So I phoned him and his wife answered the phone – he was in bed! He brought his rifle to the house and blew off the snake's head.

Many years later, in our garden in Gweru, we still had problems with snakes, cobras in particular. We had a Jack Russell terrier who was a great snake catcher. He had a sister, and one day in the garden Margaret saw them tugging at a snake which they had caught and bitten in two. It was still full of fight even though half its body was ten yards away. She saw Taffy, the male dog, shake himself and showers of something leaving his body. We could only assume it was snake venom as there was no other explanation. There is a spitting cobra called an Egyptian cobra, or Ringhals, and this was one of them. Margaret entertained the snake whilst I sneaked up behind it with a brick and killed it. From the word go, Margaret had learned to keep a snake's attention by moving in front of it whilst I found a suitable weapon with which to despatch it. All this from a town girl from Londonderry!

Taffy tackled one too many snakes and was bitten by a banded cobra which he killed but too late. He died a few minutes later in our kitchen. A very sad end to a faithful friend. He had killed six cobras altogether.

At the same house Margaret was sweeping the passage and had to brush out a small snake as if it were an everyday event.

In Mutare we had a visitation from a snake in an unusual way. We had a minister from the Mount Zion Fellowship in Jerusalem, named Gary Fox, staying with us and ministering in our church. One evening, as he was having a bath, he shouted, "There is a snake in the bath!" Fortunately he was out of the bath drying himself and had let the water out. The snake came up through the drain pipe and had its head on the side of the bath with its tail still down the drain pipe. It was easily despatched and we went to bed. When did you last have a bath with a snake?

The next day, Margaret hung some bath towels on an expanding wall rack over the bath, which could be pulled out from the wall and, when finished with, was pushed back against the wall again. This day, as she removed the towels, a snake was curled up behind them on the bath. It was the same type that had visited us the day before and was probably its mate. I think they were brown house snakes, which are harmless

One of the few international evangelists, Reinhard Bonnke, a German whose organisation was called 'Christ For all Nations' (CFaN), was ministering in Bulawayo. Whilst he was preaching he had live snakes thrown at him.

At Springvale, the farmhouse faced east and was built high up on a kopje. It had big windows facing the sun but under a verandah. It had a lovely view of a rolling hill across a valley in front of the house.

Early one morning whilst still in bed we were woken up by a mighty crash and thought a terrorist had shot at us. On investigation we found a dove on the bedroom floor. Since the bedroom faced east we can only assume the dove had seen a reflection of the sun and hills in the window which somehow had fooled it. It was that time of the morning.

A strange incident happened. At the dairy about one hundred yards away there was an electrical leak at certain times of the day; one had a definite, but not deadly, shock when putting milk churns into a fridge. I called out an electrician from the government Electricity Supply Commission for some unrelated reason. Whilst standing on a chair in the kitchen and working on an electric control box he was suddenly hit by an almighty shock which practically threw him off the chair. He let out some vociferous expletives for which he later apologised. What had happened was that our cook had switched on the grill on the stove and this caused the shock. It was discovered that the stove was incorrectly wired; when the grill was switched on it was connected to the earth wire which was in turn connected to the water pipe system for better earthing. The water pipe was connected to the large water storage tank on a rise above the house which in turn was connected to the water supply down to the dairy. This supply was connected to the fridges which became alive when the grill was switched on in the kitchen. The workers used to stand on sacks to minimise the effect of the current when they put milk churns into the fridge. They were only too happy when we solved the problem.

After four years we left this farm and bought our own place a few miles away also near Bulawayo. It was a dairy farm with the same climate that we had been used to for eight years. It lay in the twenty five inch rainfall belt which I had learned to cope with (as opposed to thirty five inches in Mashonaland). We started off well and had a good first year. Then things started to go wrong. I had bought most of my basic dairy cows from a well-known farmer and a friend of mine. Some months after we started I noticed none of my cows were breeding. It turned out that the seller's cows were suffering from a disease called 'Vibrio Foetus' which prevented cows from conceiving for eighteen months. Added to this we experienced two years of serious drought with our rainfall reduced to ten inches in two years instead of fifty.

We survived this with much debt so when we had a good fourth year and paid off all our debts, we decided to sell the farm, having four children. It was a wise move. We had a number of scary incidents before we sold. Margaret had driven to our neighbours with her cousin Hazel, arrived from Belfast. On her way back she had an accident in our vehicle, a Morris Oxford station wagon. Turning right into our driveway, a car driven by a one-eyed man who was travelling from Lusaka tried to overtake her on the right, saw that she was turning right and switched to overtake her on the left. He couldn't make it and caught her a glancing blow on the left of the vehicle.

The station wagon turned around and rolled over twice, landing on its roof. I was milking at the time close by and heard the crash. When I arrived I found Pip walking down the road, having been thrown out of the side glass window without a scratch on him. Margaret, seven months pregnant with Tim, climbed out where the windscreen had been. Brian was strapped in a seat in the front between driver and passenger and was hanging up-side down. Joy was still in the back of the vehicle. Hazel managed to climb out in spite of a spinal injury. They were all covered with egg yolk since Hazel had a dozen eggs on her lap which they had brought from the neighbour. The eggs exploded and they were all covered in egg yolk. Since we were so short of cash at that time I only had third-party insurance meaning we lost the vehicle since it was a write-off. Fortunately we had a good friend who lent us a vehicle to tide us over.

A couple of months later I was milking early in the morning when Margaret started labour pains. She sent Joy to the dairy to call me, and since I only had two more cows to milk I finished them and then went to the house. What I didn't know was that Joy had not come straight to the dairy, being afraid of the dark or something, and I found a frantic wife. We went flat out to the hospital thirteen miles away with Margaret holding on. We reached the hospital just in time and got in the lift to go to the first floor. It was a large lift, big enough to hold a stretcher. Margaret was sitting on a seat provided for the lift operator.

We reached the floor, but Margaret had a contraction and couldn't move. I walked out, the doors closed behind me and she down she went to the ground floor again. I raced downstairs and got into the lift again. This time all went well; Margaret reached the delivery room and rang the bell. A sister was there immediately and delivered the baby who, having come so quickly, was blue and was immediately put in an oxygen tent to recover. It all happened so quickly the doctor had no time to get there. Margaret swears the baby was born before I could walk down to the ground floor. This was on Boxing Day, and what a precious boy Tim has been.

As a baby, our second child Pip had constant throat problems, and the ENT specialist took his tonsils out when he was nine months old. The surgeon became a great friend and was Pip's godfather.

10

Changing Careers

Having sold our farm, we went next door and managed the Rogers' farm again. We were well settled, being amply paid and on a pension scheme, when disaster struck again. I was given the sack!

The Rogers family all lived in each other's pockets at West Nicholson. Uncle Bert had died and left everything to his only child, Jack. Uncle Stan and his son, Ted, had no legal right to any property in the village. For some reason or other there was a family disagreement; Jack threw Uncle Stan and his son Ted out of the village and gave them title to the farm I was managing.

This action by Jack Rogers affected Uncle Stan mentally, and he was never the same again. He had lived in West Nicholson for over fifty years, and to be thrown out by his nephew was too much for him. It meant that instead of the farm carrying one European family it now had to carry three. There was no accommodation for three families so I was given three months' notice.

Now we had an extra problem. We had booked ourselves a holiday in a hotel, just south of Durban in South Africa, and were due to meet Margaret's parents there. Her father, having sold his business, was on board a ship to meet us in Durban to spend our holiday with us. Should we or should we not spend our money on a holiday when I had no job to return to?

Since Margaret's parents were committed we decided to 'throw caution to the wind' and go on holiday. All went well at first, and we enjoyed time with the parents at the seaside south of Durban in a lovely hotel called the Blue Marlin. However, after two weeks Tim started to be ill, and after a couple of days we had to call a doctor. The doctor diagnosed measles and said, "I will be kind to you, but you must go within twenty four hours; otherwise I will have to put the whole hotel into quarantine!" So we packed up and headed out for Rhodesia.

Margaret sat in the back of the car with Tim wrapped up on her lap. We decided we needed to see a doctor again and called into a hospital at Standerton. What a problem. They only spoke Afrikaans and we had great difficulty in communicating with them, but we managed somehow and arrived home safely.

Going through the last village before reaching home I called in at a newspaper shop and bought a Rhodesian Farmer magazine. I had been out of the country for three weeks and wanted to look at the job adverts. In that edition for the last time was an advert for a Land Bank Inspector. I applied, got the job, and set out on a new career at the age of forty. I stayed in that organisation for seventeen years, rising to be Regional Manager for the Midlands and Matabeleland, covering an area more than one and a half times the size of England. During this time we moved house eight times as I was promoted and sent to different districts.

In order to get promotion, I studied at home for three years and was able to become an Associate of the Chartered Institute of Secretaries, which qualification enabled senior management to promote me above many staff members who had been in office much longer than I. This caused friction between some, but it didn't faze me since I had studied while they went to the sports club. I jumped over fourteen men senior in years of service to me. Being in the position that I had now attained, I was privileged to have access to the accounts and management practices of some of the finest farmers in the world.

For example, we had fruit farmers, farming at over five to six thousand feet or more (the highest mountain in the country was over eight thousand feet above sea level but never experienced snow). To visit a fruit farmer with orchards of apples grown on the Palmette system (training the trees fan-like on wire trellises) was a sight for sore eyes. They particularly grew the Granny Smith variety but also Golden Delicious, Red Delicious, Winter Permain and many other lesser varieties. We had peach farmers producing the most fabulous fruit which was exported to Europe. Because of our geographical position our peaches matured two weeks before the South African crop so obtained high prices before the South African crop flooded the market. It was a major management technique to achieve this, going back to the date of pruning, irrigation practices and so on.

One farmer friend, Toby Micklethwaite, was in the top flight of all fruit growers (he was also a top flight cattle man farming six thousand acres) and grew the most fabulous stone fruit i.e. peaches, nectarines, apples, figs, plums and others. He had a big problem with baboons which loved his fruit, especially peaches. The havoc and destructive things they could do in an orchard were astonishing. It was heartbreaking to see the damage they would do to peach trees in full production, especially trees carrying fruit just ready for harvesting and export. They did dreadful damage to the trees themselves, breaking off the most fruitful branches by their weight and thus destroying the shape of the tree which had been pruned to get maximum production, a process taking many seasons.

Toby put an electric fence around his orchard which was effective for a while. Eventually the baboons mastered the art of wheedling their way through the live electric wires and carried on their destructive work. They were past masters at watching workers and timing their invasion whilst they were at lunch.

Toby reported his problem to the Wild Life Game Department. They decided to poison them using poisoned maize, a ready part of a baboon's diet. First they set out unpoisoned maize to get them used to it. This went on for about a week and the baboons were feeding happily on this diet. Then the Game Department put out the poisoned grain. Unfortunately, the leading dog baboon refused that day to let any other member of his troop to eat the poisoned food. He went from heap to heap and died there and then. How this could have happened no-one knew. There was a great outcry from the troop as they saw what had happened to their leader and now had to select a new one, him being the most violent of the survivors. Baboons have a bark like a dog, and they were most vigilant in their watching over their troop. A sentry was always on duty, and they always saw you before you spotted them. You knew they were around by the sentry's bark before you could see them. An amusing thought comes to mind. Listen to a tennis match at Wimbledon and listen to a linesman cry, "fault," and you will constantly hear the bark of a baboon. Uncanny but true. The call sounds just like a dog baboon on a kopje in the bush.

The fruit farmers were very generous to us. One Christmas, a farmer brought us a terrific supply of all sorts of fruit which we put in the kitchen. Half an hour later another farmer brought us an equally generous gift so we had to hide the first lot outside at the back so that there would be no embarrassment.

Other exotic crops we grew were sugar, citrus, coffee and tea. We had large sugar estates in the lowveld, particularly at Triangle and Hippo Valley where we had a large sugar refinery. Our production was such that we exported around sixty thousand tons per annum. When I first started to be involved in sugar finance I visited the estate where we had hundreds of thousands of dollars invested. I was horrified to see a large cane field on fire, worrying about the loss of our investment. There were no fire appliances around, and I couldn't understand the lack of concern in the estate. On airing my concern, my ignorance was exposed. It was a management practice to set the cane field on fire deliberately to burn off the dead cane leaves before the cane was cut so that there would be a limited amount of rubbishy leaves going through the mill. Burning did no damage to the cane stalk. Cane growers were paid out based on the weight of cane delivered and the percentage of sugar in the cane.

Coffee growing was another crop I enjoyed financing and following up. We grew the Arabica variety, being the type which is percolated. The other variety was Robusta, grown mainly by Africans in the lowveld because it required very little capital investment and not a lot of management skills. In those days, Robusta coffee was used exclusively for instant coffee.

For Arabica coffee there had to be a vigorous spraying program against leaf diseases – leaf miner and leaf spot being the worst. The coffee was graded according to bean size and flavour. Every consignment from the farm was delivered to a large storage shed or barn, a sample taken and tested by an expert coffee taster. He would percolate the sample and then take a mouthful and expel it through his nose. This is where the flavour is. After a number of tests he had to give up because his nose became raw. No wonder!

We exported nearly all our coffee and were well able to compete with our biggest rival, Kenya. Rivals also included Uganda and Brazil. Coffee is very susceptible to frost so we were always pleased to hear that Brazil had had a late and severe frost.

I was on a coffee farm one day when a swarm of locusts from nearby Mozambique approached. It was such a thick swarm it obscured the sun; had it settled on the farm it would have ruined it in twenty four hours. The farmer who was a great friend of mine was prepared for such an event, fired prepared grass on the contours, beat tins and seemed to keep the locusts away. It took them thirty minutes to fly over the property, and they settled for the night on a ranch two miles away. Locusts can be sprayed and killed at the hopper stage before they can fly, but the Mozambique government had neither the will nor the expertise to do so. It was too sophisticated an operation for them.

Tea production was another fascinating crop to grow. Tea growers were out-growers contracted to a factory which had to be very close by. Tea was grown in the Eastern Highlands, the climate being suitable for coffee and tea production. Tea comes from a bush which growers plant close together to form a hedge. When plucking begins (you pluck tea, pick cotton, reap maize and tobacco, harvest fruit, combine wheat) a level top is created sometimes using a hedge cutter to create a level growing base. Tea shoots then appear, growing straight up like salt cellars. The plucker – always a woman – then takes two leaves and a bud and throws them into a basket carried on her back.

This is the best shoot to pluck; anything more than two leaves and a bud diminishes the quality of the end product. Some retailers call their product 'Two Leaves Tea' and have a logo on their packet to demonstrate it. Of course it is not always possible to maintain this as many shoots carry three leaves but the art of management is to catch the majority of growth at the two leaves stage. If there are four leaves the trained plucker will throw them on the ground.

It is important to negotiate with the factory management for them to receive your tea. The factory has to be close to the grower so that he can deliver his truckload of green leaves before they start to ferment on the truck or tractor trailer. The vehicle is weighed full on a large scale and then weighed empty on return. The green leaves are spread out on a moving belt which takes them to a cutter, having been dried with hot air whilst on the slowly moving belt which feeds the green leaves into the cutters. The cut leaf is then further dried until all moisture is driven out. It passes into a large grading unit with about seven different sizes of sieves, the last one being the producer of the highest quality. The top quality tea was called 'Peko Fannings' and the next one, as I recall, was 'Golden Orange Peko' – sounds a bit like of Chinese origin.

There were four factories in this area, all fairly close to the Mozambique border. Tea never lost its colour in the field, and it was always a lovely sight in winter to see a green hillside in contrast to the dry veld. I knew the manager of one factory very well and always bought his top quality tea from him, a couple of pounds at a time. By the way, if you ever see beige-coloured leaves floating in your tea know that that is a very poor quality tea since they are dead leaves which have been too old to survive the curing process. They come out at the end of the grading machine and have been deliberately added to save costs.

There was no problem in marketing our tea; most of it was exported.

11

Farming in the Lowveld

I loved Rhodesian agriculture.

An unusual farming venture came across my path. A Christian dairy farmer friend also produced honey on a commercial scale. It was a major programme with him having eight hundred hives around the area. They had to be kept in special small houses which were locked to keep out thieving Africans who had a very sweet tooth. They loved to suck pieces of sugar cane whilst walking down the street, spitting out the sucked pieces onto the pavement – a very unhealthy practice.

The houses also had small entrance holes to keep out honey badgers which could devastate a hive in minutes. Also, every hive had to stand in water to keep ants out. At our house in Salisbury we frequently saw swarms of bees stopping in an area of avocado trees. My friend brought swarm-catching boxes and set them up in the trees. He caught numerous swarms, collecting them at night once a week or so since he was always looking for new material. It was strange how our property became a channel for swarms on a regular basis, but after a couple of months they dried up. He travelled round at night visiting other places with lots of full and empty swarm-catching boxes. Dedicated farming indeed! He deserved to succeed and he did.

He was an expert tracker of terrorists when on 'call up'. He was involved in the capture of a major terrorist leader at night, setting up what they called 'a killing ground', an area where if anyone entered they were immediately shot by men in an ambush. This time the man was captured first but the rest of his followers killed. Such was life in those days – life and death at the same time.

My friend had a place like a hospital clinic; he produced a large quantity of honey in hospital-like clean conditions, and his equipment for extracting and storing honey was all of stainless steel. He exported all his honey to Germany in forty-five gallon drums. Apparently there were certain international standards to be met regarding quality – a scientific test for which my friend's honey qualified easily. My son, Brian, went to stay with him on a school project to do with farming. This was in the Mazoe valley area.

African bees were the black variety – vicious and dangerous and not good honey producers. These attacked the more docile brown bees which produced much better honey per hive. I once saw a newspaper article which said that some African black bees had been sent to the southern states of America for scientific purposes; some had escaped and had started killing local species. It showed a map of their progress across the country which was quite devastating to local producers. That was many, many years ago, and I have heard nothing more since. They also affected seed crop production.

They were naturally angry and aggressive beasts and without provocation would attack humans, animals and dogs with even chickens not being immune from their stings. My neighbour at Heany kept a hive near his house but had to dispose of it because of their habit of stinging visitors.

One of our major events which I was involved in was the growing of wheat and cotton in the Sabi Valley, Sabi being the name of a major river flowing into the Zambezi in Mozambique. A large dam was thrown up about a hundred miles upstream from the valley to feed water downstream for irrigation. I think it took three weeks for water released from the dam to reach the valley. Obviously, this depended on the time of the year. In the valley there were twenty-three farmers with four hundred acres each of irrigated land. They grew wheat in winter and cotton in summer on the same piece of ground. The soils were excellent for growing these crops under irrigation, being alluvial and at least ninety feet deep.

The valley was in the lowveld and extremely hot in summer. Irrigation was essential and unusual techniques were used. The river could not be kept flowing all the time so the water was pumped or extracted from the sand in the river bed, the sand being twenty feet deep or more in parts. Specially designed sand pumps were sunk many feet deep into the sand which held the water. It was pumped into specially designed irrigation channels, and the farmers pumped it out as required. The land was very flat so overhead irrigation was essential. A major electricity grid was built, for all pumps had to be electric. All the houses were supplied with electricity – very necessary since air conditioning was essential with temperature reaching forty degrees celsius. The AFC was only involved in financing the crops. Major investment had been poured in to build twenty-three houses with all mod-cons. Servants' quarters, water supply, etc. had to be built first and this in a remote area of the lowveld. Hundreds of tons of cement and thousands of bricks had to be transported by road to complete the estate. Miles of irrigation channels going past each farm were made of cement and a huge pump house to control the water supply was constructed with a major switchboard to control water supply to the farmers. All this was done before we got involved. Of course, each farm had its own pump house with a meter.

The wheat seed was planted by aircraft specially designed for crop spraying and seed sowing. The whole planting and spraying operation had to be extremely well planned to avoid planting or spraying the same area twice or even missing an area altogether. Workers were given flags on poles to wave and set at equal distances in long lines to guide the aircraft on each run. The pilot had to land at frequent intervals to restock seed or chemicals. I once stood under a crop sprayer and was amazed at the down-draught, the force of the chemicals being sprayed. Once was enough; it was too dangerous to be covered in chemicals more than once. The workers wore special protective clothing. I did the same under a wheat seeding operation and again was amazed at the force of wheat seed hitting the ground. The wheat crop was all harvested by combine harvesters and transported about a hundred miles to the nearest Grain Marketing Board Depot. It provided good business for local transporting companies.

There were eleven thousand acres involved in this one valley, all in one continuous line, so you can imagine the importance to the local communities and the influence on the social structure in what was a remote, undeveloped area of Rhodesia. Cotton growing demanded a high level of management. First the wheat straw had to be removed – usually by burning, there being no other economical way of disposing of it since it had no value as cattle feed. The cotton land was heavily watered before planting by machine and then watered heavily again. Once the seed germinated, from then on water was withheld for six weeks forcing the roots to follow the retreating water level thus developing a large root system to feed on a good nutrient supply. Temperatures would rise to forty degrees celsius. Cotton growth was prodigious and yields were very satisfactory, making the venture very profitable.

Cotton picking was done by hand, providing a major cash injection into the local village economy. Because of this our cotton commanded a high price on the world market. I did see one cotton picking machine, but they had tremendous drawbacks. The machine picked up an awful lot of trash thus reducing the value of the end product, since the cotton had now to be cleaned by machine, a process not necessary with hand-picked cotton. It had the disadvantage of having to let the whole plant come to maturity so losing some production to cotton fallout.

The crop was sprayed from the air, but this did not have to be so. Some growers used the old, cheaper system of using knapsack sprayers which were very effective but time consuming. Spraying was necessary because pests such as boll worm, cotton stainer (an insect which secreted a red dye into the cotton boll thus ruining the white lint), aphids and leaf miners would reduce yields and quality. Much profit was to be made by good growers, one grower paying $75,000 in income tax in one year of wheat and cotton production. Production of agricultural crops in this lowveld climate was prodigious when irrigated. I saw a pawpaw tree eighteen months old with eighty large pawpaws on it – excellent yield indeed. Another grower planted thirty acres of bananas and 'made a killing'.

Local villages had booming shops because of the hundreds of thousands of dollars earned in cash by the hundreds of cotton pickers employed. I cannot remember any labour disputes arising because their income was vital for their families, food, clothing, school fees and so on. All the growers paid good wages and soon lost labour if they defaulted in any way.

The Sabi river had numerous large pools of water, and in one pool I counted thirty nine Hippos with young as well. Hippos were a menace as they are graziers and came out at night and grazed on the wheat.

An enterprise in which I was not involved was the Mazoe Valley Citrus Estate. A dam was built on the Mazoe river to irrigate hundreds of acres of oranges (and other citrus fruit) to produce orange squash. This was not far from Harare, as it is now called, and was highly successful, exporting its produce all over southern Africa. The orange skins were dried and ground up for including in dairy stock feed.

In Triangle and Hippo Valley, citrus fruit was also produced. The grapefruit grew so large they were too big for raw consumption, housewives finding them too big for their family table and producers also finding resistance by other countries when exported. Instead, they were manufactured into grapefruit juice and canned grapefruit pieces.

Soya beans and groundnuts were grown in quantity and exported. Sunflowers were grown for their cooking oil with the residue of sunflower seed cake meal used for cattle feed. Other crops of huge importance were tobacco and maize which earned large amounts of foreign exchange, a valuable commodity in a third world country which was trying to 'keep up with the Joneses' in foreign affairs.

Some of our agriculture production was world class. For example, my father would grow just over four tons of winter wheat per acre in eleven months. In Rhodesia an excellent farmer would grow nine tons – five of maize followed by four of wheat – on the same ground in a year.

Our Rattray Research Station bred an excellent maize variety called SR 52. It was bred for the highveld and needed a long growing season – a hundred and fifty days or more – for maximum yields. It was every maize grower's dream to belong to the '5 ton club', meaning he had produced fifty bags per acre. Under irrigation in Matabeleland I grew forty nine bags and missed the target. Rattray produced other hybrid varieties suitable for low rainfall areas, dry land crops in the twenty five inch rainfall belt. His work revolutionised maize production.

We had some excellent dairy farmers. A friend milked six hundred cows three times a day, one of the biggest herds in the world. We had many others, perhaps not quite so big but eminently successful. One farmer had three sons, all excellent dairymen, in the one area.

Cattle ranching in Matabeleland was of major importance and was the main enterprise over hundreds of thousands of acres. Diseases had to be constantly under control by regular weekly or fortnightly dipping, in some cases, depending on the time of the year. Foot and mouth was a menace because it was carried by buffalo, eland, kudu and other wide-ranging, cloven-hoofed game animals. When diagnosed, the only way we could stop it spreading amongst domestic stock was by inoculation. This had to be carried out by the Veterinary Department, a Government organisation.

I have found beef meat in England to be tasteless and characterless. Give my wife a sirloin or topside or silverside or aitchbone or a roll from one of my two-year olds, straight off the veld in April, and you will know what beef should taste like!

In September every year Bulawayo held its Agriculture Show, and since Bulawayo was the centre of the cattle industry, beef stock played a great part in the Show. There was serious competition for pens of ten stall-fed steers which, at the end of the Show, were auctioned off to butchers. There had been no green grass for five months so all show animals were pen-fed. We exported ten thousand tons of beef per annum to the European Union.

It was always a joy, when you walked into your butcher's in September, to be offered 'show beef' – beef I can assure you of the highest quality, covered in a lovely layer of fat. Yum yum! That's character for you! In this country – and elsewhere – there seems to be a campaign against eating animal fat. Phooey, I say! I have eaten fried egg, bacon, fried bread, dip, pork sausages, pork chops with a lovely layer of fat around them, cream in my tea, cornflakes and puddings – you name it – and I take no medicine on a daily basis ever.

Fattening bullocks, steers, oxen – call them what you will – or unwanted heifers was one of my favourite practices. All our cattle were slaughtered at an abattoir in Bulawayo on a guaranteed weight and grade basis, but you could opt to sell them by auction on the open market. Prices were set out for a year ahead, the prices changing weekly. The lowest price was at the end of the rains, April, then gradually increasing as the grass quality diminished and artificial feeding became necessary but then more expensive. It was always a great challenge to produce 100% top grade animals at the highest price before the new season set in and grass began to grow again. Early November was my choice, hoping to get the animals out of the pens before they became waterlogged.

The greatest challenge was to have every animal graded 'Rhodesia Best', commanding the top guaranteed price. They had to be four-tooth – a problem because you could put a four-tooth animal in the pens but the very act of pen-feeding them could bring up more teeth prematurely. I grew all my own food for up to one hundred steers at a time.

Only once did I get it right in six years of trying. On being slaughtered they were graded on the hook by a government grader. I was lucky at my most successful slaughtering when the grader pointed out that one carcase was a marginal case but added, "Because you are interested in your job I will give you the benefit of the doubt." Otherwise, he said, he would have given me a lower grade. 100% for a hundred animals was a dream achieved only once – but how satisfying. The number of animals I could feed varied every year and was based on the rains and the amount of feed I could grow

Feeding heifers was easier. They pen-fed very successfully. The usual feeding time was ninety days. Cattle had to be booked in for slaughter at least three months in advance to get a slaughter date. The abattoir slaughtered four hundred animals per day, every day of the year, except Sunday. The Cold Storage Commission had massive ranches and held thousands of stock to maintain a regular throughput, bringing in their own stock when necessary to maintain slaughter numbers. Quite an organisation! They also 'farmed out' cattle to acceptable ranchers. The farmer did not have to pay for them and had to market the stock through the CSC – a very good scheme to help farmers who lacked the capital to buy stock. All CSC cattle were branded for identification and, in order not to ruin the hide, all their cattle were branded on the cheek. The CSC would also buy a farmer's stock, brand them and pass them on to others. Interest was charged on your account and all income from slaughter retained until the account was cleared.

The CSC had teams of employees going around the country with branding irons in the boot. Thousands of cattle were involved every year, and the industry was well under control. Except where CSC cattle were involved, you could always sell on the open market, that is, through weekly auction sales in the larger towns.

In the lowveld where ranches were large, one hundred thousand acres or more and very far from a big town, the auctioneers went to the farmers and auctioned their stock in specially constructed sale pens close to their ranches. Transporting them from the sale pens then became the buyer's problem. Practically all cattle sold in the lowveld special sales were weaners. This was so because lions, leopards and hyenas could thin out your herd very quickly if you did not dispose of them as soon as possible. Lowveld weaner sales were an integral annual part of the farming calendar.

Due to the very hot climate the breed of cattle chosen was extremely important. Your exotic Herefords, Sussex, Aberdeen Angus, Red Poll, etc. never did well in such heat. The most adaptable were Brahmins and Afrikanders, a South African breed, the cows having large horns to fight off leopards trying to take their calves.

Local breeds such as Tulis and Shonas were bred for their ability to survive in hot, dry conditions, but being very small there was little demand in the market.

Lowveld ranchers learned to make elephant passages fenced as roadways down to rivers to direct them away from their own fencing; otherwise elephants could ruin paddock control and herds would soon be mixed up. Elephants soon learned to use them, as did other smaller species, especially giraffe, buffalo, bush buck and water buck. I saw a kudu leap over an eight foot game fence from a standing start – a magnificent sight. Impala were prolific breeders and they used the channels too.

Ranching in the lowveld included managing game too. One rancher I visited had built a canning factory; he slaughtered buffalo, canned the meat and sold it as dog food.

At West Nicholson, there was a very large meat processing factory, Liebigs, which processed more of the African breeds and produced canned bully beef as its main product.

12

Agricultural Finance

This chapter returns to some earlier events that have not been discussed so far.

I joined the staff of what was then called the Land Bank as a farm inspector in November 1963. It is now called the Agriculture Finance Corporation (AFC). It immediately became obvious that it was well organised and planned to serve the farming community in matters of finance, in spite of comments made by the obviously uninformed. It operated within a well-established legal system which controlled marketing debt collection through a stop order system with all loans registered against the title deeds of the farm so that in the case of default, monies owed could be legally collected from the sale of a property. When a farmer wanted finance he completed an application form, declaring his last two years' crop results and any other source of income like cattle sales, milk production and so on.

He also had to declare his financial position, bank overdraft and so on, the reason why he wanted money (for example, for his crop programme) etc. It has to be noted that the finances came from the government and were therefore public money from the taxpayer, hence the cautious approach adopted by management when handing out money and the security demanded. Our operations were controlled by an Act of Parliament.

It was the inspector's job to visit the farm and discuss the programme, discuss the finances to see if they were adequate or not and make agreed changes. The job also included inspection of the state of the buildings, conservation programme, fencing, dams, boreholes, condition of cattle and all facilities, the state of the homestead, roads and so on, to get a relevant assessment of the farmer's management.

A valuation of the farm was then calculated, assessing the condition of the arable land and its soil type, its state of conservation protection, fencing, roads, dams, potential arable land and the grazing land and its type. Was there bush encroachment and was the farm potential being used to capacity? Was the equipment adequate to fulfil the programme and, if not, could he afford to borrow more money to buy more equipment?

No application was a walkover. At the end of one's written report a character assessment of the farmer had to be made. One inspector finished his gloomy forecast with a cheerful comment that on this farm one crop never failed — she was pregnant again! Guidelines were adopted so that every inspector was working from a standard position. These had been adopted after many years of experience. Generally our valuations were about 80% of the estimated commercial value and guided us in the amount we would lend a farmer to purchase a new farm.

Many years later I fell foul of Ian Smith, our Prime Minister at the time, who was selling a farm which he grossly overvalued. All my figures were checked and were found to be in line with our normal practices so he didn't get his way.

I was always happy with our conservative approach. On the whole we expected a farmer to contribute 50% of capital long term estimates. This calculation did not include current crop expenses but covered purchase of farm equipment and other capital developments. First class security was demanded, chiefly the surrender of the farm title deeds.

When trained by an experienced inspector you were then given a specific area to be responsible for.

The agricultural set up in Rhodesia was excellent since much guesswork was eliminated by regulation. We had boards to control crop pricing. For example, the Grain Marketing Board controlled the marketing of maize, soyabeans, groundnuts and sorghum. The Tobacco Marketing Board controlled Virginia, Burley and Turkish tobacco. Cotton, coffee and milk were all governed the same way. It was illegal to sell these crops to anyone else unless legal permission was obtained. Some farmers in the lowveld close to the South African border exported their produce – mostly citrus, which grew prolifically in the heat and under irrigation. It was quite a game to recover the money since we had no legal authority to obtain the money in South Africa.

Mr Vincent von Memerty, General Manager of the Land Bank at the time, was instrumental in bringing in legislation known as the 'Stop Order Act' which forced all these boards to keep a register of all sellers and to register a stop order against their income from sales to that organisation. It meant that when we advanced money for the growing of tobacco the Tobacco Marketing Board was legally bound to remit money from the grower's sales to us until the value of the stop order was fulfilled. This gave tremendous security to the lender.

If the farmer came up with a scheme which lay outside the norm he would have difficulty in raising money. Many organisations used this system, especially the commercial banks, to do business with farmers. It gave them a wide range of choices to do business as they wanted. It spread the financial risks involved in agriculture and commerce.

Tobacco was very susceptible to damage or even destruction by hail, a common feature of the weather in Rhodesa. Insurance companies arranged for crop insurance, which was a great boon and protection for farmers. It could turn out to be very profitable, especially if the crop was virtually written off. Payment by the insurance company was very favourable, meaning the farmer did not have to reap, cure, grade and market his crop. One greedy farmer anticipated or faked a hail storm by arming his employees with sticks in which he had driven nails. He then sent his workers out to beat the crop with these sticks hoping to simulate a hail storm. The insurance inspector was suspicious and called the police. The farmer was given no pity and was jailed.

Some farmers struck it lucky. Tobacco is a resilient weed and would start to grow again, giving the farmer a second but lesser crop. The insurance company put an age limit of sixty on every borrower, no matter what his programme, and if he was over that age he would have to make his own insurance arrangements. It was different from hail insurance which was only available to tobacco farmers. All farmers' loans came under an insurance policy called mortgage insurance, meaning all their loans were covered and if they died before they were sixty their AFC loans were repaid in full, no matter what the amount.

In Mutare, years later, we had a tragic case when a farmer disguised his true age and took five years off on his application form so that we would not take his age into account when considering his application. He was in financial difficulties but was holding his own yet not decreasing his level of debt. He needed more land, his own farm being too small to service his debt more swiftly. When the next door farm came up for sale we did detailed calculations of his increased debt burden to see whether it would be financially viable for us to help him buy the farm. It seemed positive so we helped him buy the farm even though his debt load was high. He was a good farmer and had learned from his previous lack of financial nous. He was busy working on his new farming programme when he died. I went straight out to see his widow and assure her of our continued support during this difficult time. I said she would be financially well off since he was fifty eight and all his loans would be repaid by the mortgage insurance. I was appalled when she said he was sixty three so none of his debt would be repaid. We had to sell the farms and all the equipment to recover our loans, and she was left penniless. She had no idea he had falsified his age. Tragic...

We moved from Bulawayo to Gweru in January 1964 where the Land Bank decided to locate its Headquarters for Matabeleland and the Midlands since it would be more centrally situated for administrative purposes. I was then given my own area to service and so started a successful career in Agricultural Finance. I covered very diverse farming production: excellent dairy farmers (some of the finest in the country), maize and groundnut growers, cattle ranchers, irrigation farmers growing acres of wheat, maize and cotton, sugar, citrus and market gardening.

One of my clients achieved the right to be a member of the ten ton club reaping over fifty bags to the acre of maize – a truly magnificent sight to see such production. On the same land he followed up with a crop of wheat yielding fifty bags per acre on very heavy, black cotton soils (greenstone schists to the uninitiated). Land preparation was vital, getting the timing right between one crop and another. He grew winter wheat which was susceptible to frost in its early stage soon after germination.

Agricultural Finance

Leaf and stem rust were a problem, but our scientist produced hybrid resistant varieties.

One of the major pests in respect of wheat growing was the quelea bird. They are seed eaters about the size of a sparrow, gathered in flocks of hundreds of thousands and roosted at night always in the same place. They could devastate any seed crop in hours if left to themselves, wheat particularly. The only defence the large scale wheat grower had was to kill them at their roosting place. This was done at night by spraying them from the air with a liquid called Quelatox by aircraft specially designed for the purpose. On one such spraying event the pilot misjudged the time and arrived too early. When he started spraying the whole flock rose up en masse and suddenly surrounded his aircraft in their thousands – a phalanx of frantic birds which entered his cockpit, knocking off his face mask which was there to protect him from the poisonous spray, knocking off an external fuel tank which we found in the farmer's dip tank the next day and forcing the pilot to retreat. Although spraying was repeated all over the country to protect wheat and other seed crops, I never heard of one with such drastic consequences as this. It was at a town called Kwekwe, between Bulawayo and Harare.

In Gweru we bought our first house with money borrowed from the AFC – on very favourable terms, being a member of staff. (This was the first of a number of properties we bought and made profits on.) There we began to experience the change from rural life to urban life and the effect it had on the children. Attending a large school exposed them to all the normal children's diseases, colds and flu. Joy caught chicken pox and Tim whooping cough. The weather in Gweru did not help; it was much colder in winter than we were used to in Bulawayo. In 1965 we had children in junior school and nursery school.

We had a cat which found someone's pigeon cote; he would bring a pigeon into the house in the middle of the night and eat it under our bed, night after night. We never discovered who it was that was losing the birds!

Now I decided to push for promotion into management, and I set myself to study the subjects which would help me to achieve that - Law, Economics, Accountancy and English. For my first English exam paper I was awarded first prize in all southern Africa – quite a surprise! In the house we agreed a disciplined timetable to help me study in the evenings. We had four children, and they co-operated wonderfully by allowing me peace every night for two hours. I studied most Saturday afternoons instead of going to the sports club, and this contributed to my progress. We did this for three years, and I was able to pass all my exams in those years. Credit must go to my family for this.

At the end of 1968 I was transferred on promotion to Salisbury where I was gradually introduced to management requirements. The basic work was interviewing farmers and potential clients as to the standards of management and finances needed to negotiate a loan. I was trained to take hold of an applicant's file, hold it up and say to myself, "What can I do to help this farmer?" It also involved advising senior management of the amount of money to be granted, what conditions to impose and the securities required to make the loan legal. This offer would be put to the applicant who then had the prerogative of accepting or rejecting the offer. I was a member of the Mashonaland West branch of the AFC which was the centre of tobacco and maize production and considerable soya bean and ground nut production too.

We had three branches in the AFC: the one already mentioned and the Mashonaland East and Matabeleland branches. The West branch involved more financial investment than the other branches. This was because of its higher and more consistent rainfall and smaller farms and because they were more intensive and therefore did not need the greater number of acres. As the rainfall was relatively more reliable, it was a safe place for us in which to invest.

As a consequence we were able to start a Tenant Farming Scheme. This was a very dangerous enterprise from the lender's point of view because it had no security in the land in case of failure. However, we devised a scheme whereby we gathered information from local successful farmers about the suitability of certain farm managers who showed capability and the desire to branch out alone but lacked the capital to buy their own property. Provided such a farm manager could satisfy our requirements of available finance and have a record of success as a manager in the programme he proposed, we would grant him the necessary finance. We had a good success rate, and I cannot remember any failure in our contribution towards promoting agricultural development.

13

Mashonaland East

After two years of management training and active involvement in management, I was transferred on promotion to our Umtali office in the Eastern Highlands part of the Mashonaland East branch.

The ecology was different (being more tropical); there we grew coffee and tea, sugar and many market gardening crops and fruit such as pineapples and raspberries for canning. It was my introduction to a fruit called 'Pompelmuus' which appeared to be a cross between grapefruit, lemon and orange – the point being that it made excellent marmalade which we enjoyed for breakfast every day.

Guavas grew wild near the town of Chipinge, and these became a good contribution to our diet. The most significant tree was the Baobab, which had a huge trunk and then small branches above. It looked as if it was growing upside-down. Its fruit had a very acidic flavour – very distinctive – but its name escapes me. Some had a tree trunk so huge you could make a room inside it. When the fruit dried naturally the seeds inside made it a good children's rattle.

Manicaland, as the area was called, was famous for its Msasa trees. In spring their leaves were coloured like in an English autumn – the most beautiful russets and reds and pinks imaginable. To see a hillside (kopje) dressed in these colours was always a stunning sight. They then turned green for the rest of the summer.

A lovely film was made locally called simply 'Msasa Time', travelling around Manicaland and highlighting the beauty of the various spring colours.

We helped one farmer to grow mushrooms and eventually helped him to build a canning factory on his farm. These crops were new to me, and there was a lot to learn. But it was good to have one's mind challenged by new enterprises. In the beginning, coffee and tea financing was not a significant part of our financial investment portfolio, but it grew dramatically and they became significant contributors to the local and national economy.

I have described in some detail elsewhere the growing of wheat and cotton but now, as sub-manager of the branch, I was seriously responsible for carrying out management policy in this area of what was called Middle Sabi. It was fascinating work, and I revelled in the experience I was getting. The farmers involved were specially selected and were competent young men. All were married, and their homes had to have air conditioning because this was lowveld and very, very hot. Fruit and bananas grew almost minute by minute when properly watered and managed.

After my father died my mother came out in 1972; I took her down to the Sabi Valley and had lunch with a lady from Shrewsbury, much to the lady's delight. I also showed mother coffee and tea farms to give her some idea of what Africa could produce.

Middle Sabi was an isolated area and many of the farmers bought their own aeroplanes to get to Salisbury some three hundred miles away. One such very successful farmer flew his family on holiday to South Africa but crashed into some hills near Louis Trichardt just south of the border killing everyone on board – a tragic result of success.

I became very friendly with one young coffee grower who was a dropout from Durban University but had applied himself vigorously to coffee farming and had amazed everyone with his success. He bought the next door farm, expanded into growing Burley tobacco and bought a half share in an aeroplane with the local bank manager. He also went into horse racing, owning a couple, and played polocrosse. His wife was a blond hotel receptionist and became a winning tobacco grower in her own right. Tragically he too killed himself at Fort Victoria when returning from South Africa. They had no children.

My Branch Manager went on leave and I was promoted Acting Manager for the month he was away. This meant living in an hotel in Salisbury during the week and coming home on Friday evening – a three hour drive home and the same on a Monday morning back again. The senior management at head office were excellent, intelligent men, and I was always happy to be in their company, always learning how they thought in order to improve my own contribution to the efficiency of the organisation.

It was in April 1973 that my life took a dramatic turn for the better. We had always brought our children up to go to church, believing it was the right thing to do. Margaret was brought up a Methodist in Londonderry, and her parents were firm Methodist members, her father being very prominent in church affairs. I was Anglican but with no conviction.

When we moved to Salisbury in 1968 we bought a five acre property right next door to a lovely Presbyterian church so, being within walking distance, we joined that church. I think it was because we were regular attendees that I was ordained an elder, which office I took with me to Umtali in 1971.

Our attitude to our faith was rather full of pride: of course I deserved to be an elder! Was I not a manager in the AFC? Were not my children well behaved and disciplined, and did we not set a good example to the community by being seen in church and being involved in other church activities? Did we not all put something into the collection plate? Surely we had good credentials, and I considered we qualified for my appointment! The children enjoyed the youth programmes, Boys' Brigade and Girls' Brigade, and the uniforms they wore. What outstanding Christians we were!

We took this attitude with us to Umtali and served in the church there. On returning home from Salisbury one Thursday evening (it was the Easter weekend) after dinner that night Margaret asked if I minded if she took the children to a meeting in the city. The 'Youth With A Mission' (YWAM) team were visiting, and she wanted to take the children to their meeting. I said I would like to go too since I did not want to be separated from the kids having been away all week.

That was one of the best decisions of my life. At the meeting full of young people they were singing joyful songs and choruses, finishing off with "He is Lord, He is Lord" and raising their hands. This was too much for me. How could they be so familiar with a Holy God? 'Familiarity breeds contempt' I had been taught, and I refused to raise my hands.

On the Easter Monday night we went to a meeting in the Assemblies of God church where they had a visiting speaker. He was an American with a remarkable testimony. His name was Randy Pike, and he had lost the use of his legs from polio when he was fourteen. He walked with two leg irons and elbow crutches. He felt called to move from America to Australia where he was involved in a Russian refugee camp. He then moved to Johannesburg where he became Secretary to the Christian Mission to the Communist World, a Baptist organisation. That Monday night he preached a most joyful sermon, thumping the ground with his metal foot in his enthusiasm. I was so taken with his attitude I went up to him after the service and asked him why I, with all my physical faculties intact, did not have the same joy.

He asked me if I had Christ in my heart. This baffled me because I had never heard of such a thing despite having been a regular churchgoer for years. He said that was the difference between us. I protested I had been an elder in the church for years, but this was something new. He asked me if I would like to pray. There was a deadly silence; I had never prayed out loud in my life (I was forty-eight). He recognised the situation and suggested we pray together; he told me to repeat the words after him. The words were to ask the Lord Jesus to forgive me all my sins and to invite Him into my heart to be my Saviour forever. I did this and can testify I have never been the same person since then. I cannot remember the sequence of events that evening, but all three boys said the same prayer, Joy not being there as she was out with friends.

It has been said that I had a 'Damascus Road experience' which is probably correct since the next day I was different. The next day I had to go to Chipinge, around a hundred and twenty miles away, on business; on the journey I rolled the window of the car down and, with my right hand pointing to the sky, sang and shouted, "He is Lord!" for two hours, cars passing the other way wondering what on earth was going on! I could tell them! I was born again and have never lost my enthusiasm and excitement for the Lord Jesus Christ ever since.

Four years later I saw Randy Pike again in Harare and took the opportunity to introduce myself. He said, "I remember you; you were an elder in the Presbyterian Church in Umtali. I was praying for you yesterday." He was pleased to hear of my progress in my Christian life. What a wonderful example he set!

Snakes Alive

14

Civil War Years

In 1974 we were posted back to Salisbury and back to our old home in the suburb of Greencroft where we had a five acre property. I was promoted Manager of the Mashonaland East branch and took over just when war-vet activity was increasing. Farmers were being murdered in increasing numbers with unimaginable ferocity at times. One close farming friend was caught by war-vets on his property close to his house, together with his wife. In front of her they castrated him, gauged out his eyes and then hacked him to death with their small axes or demus. They then left her with her husband's mutilated body. Savagery indeed!

War-vets started to show their hands in the towns. Women suicide bombers would enter shops with explosives strapped to their thighs under their dresses. They would detonate them in the busiest areas off the shops, often blowing out plate glass windows and injuring many of those walking by with flying glass. This happened in Salisbury and Umtali.

They worked out another way to terrify people in the towns. A dozen of them would innocently enter a shop as if there to buy something, then the leader would blow a whistle and they would attack European women, knocking them to the ground, beating them, stealing their money and jewellery and handbags and, at another blast of the leader's whistle after no more than two minutes, would leave the shop, mingling with those outside and disappear before the police could arrive.

Managing the finances for the area became more and more difficult, and it was a nightmare trying to keep farmers financially viable and liquid.

Snakes Alive

I was appointed to represent the farming community on our National Security Committee because I had the widest experience and financial knowledge in the whole country. I had farmed and worked in the financial sector more than any other available person thus giving me wide experience on a national level. My personal connections with so many of the farmers and their families across the country gave me a closer understanding of the pressures they suffered and their needs. On the committee were representatives of mining, industry, tourism and commerce. We met every Monday afternoon to review the security threat in, and to, our responsible areas and could see the gradual deterioration of the security position.

The chairman was the Secretary for Agriculture, a very fine civil servant. One day in late 1977, he asked me my opinion about the general position and in specific areas. He mentioned a certain area and my reply was disturbing. I was asked what I thought we should do, and I said we should be prepared to evacuate as many farmers as possible as soon as possible. The suggestion was debated at length, and it was eventually agreed we should close down farming activity as soon as possible, the Prime Minister to be informed by the Secretary the next day. The PM never argued with the committee's recommendations, politics being ignored and reality prevailing. It was highly confidential information and a serious blow to national morale. However, facts were facts and any delay could only cost the agricultural industry more lives. So we agreed to encourage those farmers who wanted to leave to do so. In this situation I could not be gladder that I was a practising Christian.

My children wondered why I was not in the police reserve out in the bush protecting farms and properties on a regular call-out basis, as many of their school friends' fathers were doing – risking their lives for the nation. I was under an oath of secrecy not to tell anyone of my involvement in security matters and that I was debarred from call-up because of my financial experience in the agricultural industry. Not even my wife knew about it. I remember Brian once asking me why I was not contributing to police reserve activities in the field or the "sharp end" as it was called. I was not able to tell him except that I did belong to the Dad's Army branch of the police reserve which only operated at night in the towns, meaning you went back to work the next day, unlike those in the field who would be away for three weeks or more at a time, armed and ready to meet war-vets in the bush.

Every Monday night a number of us, by the invitation of the pastor of our church, gathered at the church for Bible Study and prayer. This night the pastor said we had been neglecting prayer for the country and would that night concentrate on this subject. We settled down to focus ourselves and to wait for any direction from the Lord, when one member said he had a vision. It was of a specific area in a certain province. It was exactly the area we had, at our security meeting that evening, agreed to evacuate. I was in a quandary because I was sworn to secrecy regarding the committee's deliberations. However, it seemed the Lord had His hand on the situation so after swearing them to secrecy I explained what was happening. We prayed specifically over the security situation in that region, and it appeared the Lord heard our intercession; an unusual peace fell over that area for a long time, enabling those who wanted to leave to leave without problems. For me it was a nightmare as I had to arrange finance for new farms, movement of cattle and equipment, household goods, pets and so on. It was part of my managerial responsibilities since it fell in the area I was responsible for.

Our eldest son, Pip, finished his A levels at Umtali Boys High and joined the police. Brian was next and joined the army as did Tim a year later. Pip was a fine young Christian boy who loved the Lord and would walk miles even in the rain to get to our weekly prayer meeting. He did well in the police and elected to be posted to Chipinge, a hot area in terms of security.

On the night before Joy's 21st birthday he phoned her from Chipinge but was killed the next day: 12th May 1977. It was the duty of the police to meet vehicles coming into Chipinge, mostly from South Africa, at Birchenough Bridge and escort them into Chipinge. Pip had swapped duties to oblige a friend and was on duty that morning, riding on the lead vehicle with a machine gun to protect the convoy. Quite unreasonably, he was unprotected by any armour and was totally exposed to attack. The vehicle was a Landrover owned and driven by a farmer friend of mine who volunteered the use of his time and vehicle for this purpose. He was unhurt although Pip was only six feet away. When the war-vets struck they naturally went for Pip. He was killed instantly and then the enemy fled and the convoy dispersed. No-one else was hurt. It was the last time a policeman was unprotected by armour.

We are convinced he was promoted to heaven by the Grace of God, and that night we held a victory praise meeting in our house. Although there have been times of grief, we have never faltered in our faith. Terry and Pip are rejoicing in heaven together. What a joy for them both and us too.

Much good for the Kingdom of God came out of his death even to the running of a church north of Durban. It came about as follows. When Pip was killed an office worker named Ian Jameson came and gave me his condolences. I thanked him and replied that although it was a terrible time for the family I had this great confidence that because he had been a dedicated Christian and I was too, one day we would meet again in heaven. This was my confident expectation and hope. Five years later Ian phoned me from Johannesburg and reminded me of our previous conversation. He said he had never believed a word I had said at the time but had never forgotten it. He was phoning to tell me he was now a Christian and all his family too.

As a sequel to that, fifteen years later some friends from our home church were on holiday north of Durban. One Sunday night they looked for a church to attend and found one in the vicinity. The church's pastor was Ian Jameson! Just a few sentences had great consequences.

Soon after this, in 1979, I was promoted to Regional Manager for the Midlands and Matabeleland stationed in Gweru, so we left Salisbury as it still was. I had three offices under my control at Gweru, Bulawayo and Masvingo and was responsible for agricultural finance over an area greater than England, with six inspectors to cover the area. War activity was rampant, and for two years when I left home for work my wife and I never knew if we would see each other alive again.

Travelling was dangerous but had to be done. We used armoured vehicles to go from one farm to another. I went on a trip to the lowveld, arranged by my Masvingo office to 'show the flag' and had to travel in one of them. You had to sit directly on the steel seat because if you hit a landmine a cushion under you would have the same effect as a shove ha'penny board – it could and did break your back.

On this trip I wanted to see a certain farmer who lived fifty miles off the main road. My inspector and I were armed with a rifle and a sub-machine gun, and fifty miles of dirt road on a steel seat was not the most comfortable of journeys. But the farmers had to suffer it every time they, their wives and children, left the farm. It was wild game country and we saw plenty of it, including giraffe. We also came across craters in the road where landmines had exploded. For my inspectors, it had become a commonplace expectation.

War-vets had attacked the farm we visited two days before, but the only damage they had done was to set a wardrobe on fire with an incendiary bullet. Most farmers protected their farm houses with claymore shrapnel mines which they could selectively set off when under attack. On this occasion they had failed to go off.

The Midlands area was a favourite place for Afrikaners to settle, and what a tough, courageous people they were! The war-vets had the nerve to fire on one lady, Rhona van Rensburg, as she was driving into Gweru. They missed and she jumped out of her vehicle and chased them off with her revolver!

Back at the office things were 'hotting up'. Brian was in the army in Gweru being trained as an officer. Like his father he came out with top honours and went down to the Mozambique border on anti-terrorist duty.

On one operation he lost a radio. Some months later he wanted to leave the army having fulfilled his tour of duty. They said, "Fine, but you must pay $10,000 for your lost wireless." So he phoned his mother and asked if we had that much money. She replied that there was no way that we did. However, when he showed disappointment she said, "Have you prayed about it?" He gave negative reply so she suggested that she would pray for him – which she did there and then.

Within a few days another army man phoned him from a camp a couple of hundred miles away and asked him if he had lost a wireless. Problem solved! He got out of the army 'chop chop' and went to Capetown University.

I remember well one incident that occurred around this time (in the late seventies), much to my own chagrin. It was before the fighting had stopped. We had lent a farmer some money, and I wanted to see for myself what progress he was making. This was necessary because I was due to go to a board meeting in Salisbury where all loans were open for discussion by board members – all experienced and successful farmers and not to be fooled by any fancy lending. Full details of every loan had to be declared in writing for board members to peruse. One had to be on top of your job to get through unscathed. Such was the security situation that it was deemed safer for me to fly to Salisbury rather than to go by road. We used a four-engined Viscount aircraft. On take-off it circled the airport in a tight turn until it reached ten thousand feet, then shot off to Salisbury and descended in a tight turn to land. The turn at take-off was so tight that if I sat on the right seat I could watch Margaret drive home. This had become necessary because war-vets had shot one down at Kariba by a ground-to-air missile. I would get to Salisbury and find a car waiting for me at the airport.

So before flying to Salisbury I went to this farm on the Shangani River to cover my decision to lend him money to grow Turkish tobacco. The area was not that infested by war-vets so it was worth the risk since the farmers took the same risk daily. It was some eighty miles to get there, and I was considerably disconcerted to find, just outside town, a road block put up by war-vets which the police had dismantled. So there *were* war-vets around – and active too.

It was a dirt road all the way, and war-vets were able to disguise land mines in the sandier parts of the road. It was lonely travelling, there being no habitations anywhere nearby. Indicative of this was a farm notice reading, "Meikles Ranch Homestead 10 miles," which I saw when I was passing through the top end of their eighty thousand acre ranch. No problems this time, but I had to leave by 3 o'clock to get out before dark – about a three hour journey. Just as I was about to leave, a neighbouring farmer phoned and said he would like to see me. He had rung my office and discovered I was next door. He was twenty miles further on so I had to go being so near. After all, these men and their wives and children faced these dangers daily; who was I to show fear? So I went to his farm and left at six o'clock, when just about dark.

I had an action plan should I be confronted with the enemy. On the passenger seat I had a loaded and cocked, ready-to-fire Israeli Uzzi sub-machine gun. I was driving a small BMW which was said to make a good firing platform if rolled. Where that came from I don't know, and I was baffled by the 'sense' in it. On attack my plan was to change into third, aim the car at the most people and pray for help! It was now dark, and the road surface varied from a well rolled, hard surface (one on which one could travel at a reasonable speed) to pure sand (which demanded concentration and slow driving). Hit a sandy patch at speed and you could easily roll a small car. You had to listen to the road noise to be sure you understood the road surface in the dark.

Now I was driving through open savannah veld, now heavily wooded country. Large trees and high bushes opened before me. At times I was travelling through a tunnel with my headlights boring a path in the dark. Eyes glowing now and then high in the trees revealed a 'pookie' (a small night ape); eyes lower down, close to the road revealed a hyena, jackal, small buck or wild pig. Eyes a bit higher suggested a kudu, an impala or even a buffalo. The problem was that animals frequently cross a road when lit up at night so every cell and nerve in your body was alive, reading all the signs and making sure you were not driving too fast despite the desire to get home quickly. One major mistake was to drive too fast.

All this was going through my mind. What would I do? Where was my machine gun? What sort of road surface was I travelling over? Could I go a bit faster? Every cell in my body was alive, adrenalin pumping – and then I saw them... Some men were coming down the centre of the road. Instinctively I put my foot on the brake, realised my mistake, changed into third and charged at the men, hoping to take out as many as I could before they could get me. I grabbed my machine gun in my left hand ready for anything and charged. Guess what? I nearly killed two innocent men driving some donkeys down the road. Imagination had done the rest! What they were doing at that time of night was a mystery, but it nearly ended in disaster.

Frequently, I travelled to my office in Bulawayo and found the staff coping well with the pressures, ably assisted by information coming in from farmers warning of enemy incidents in their area.

Tim also was in the army and was selected to serve in the Selous Scouts, a most efficient killing group. The internal fighting stopped in early 1980, and fears of another tragedy disappeared. Brian was discharged and went to Capetown University to study accountancy. Tim still had nine months' more service to do and would have to wait all that time now for nothing. However, it was announced by government that if you had a place at university you could, on application, be released early. The information was that it applied only to those who had a place in the local university. I discussed this with a senior member of the AFC since I was in Salisbury on business. He suggested I phone a senior officer in the army whom he knew well and said to use his name and that he was sure he would help. Tim had a place booked at Capetown University.

That is what I did and was rudely rebuffed with the information that it only applied to soldiers who had a place in the local university and not to Tim who had a place in Capetown University. I suggested I might speak to a more senior officer and was advised I could speak to the Army Commander but would get the same reply as this officer was in charge of this whole operation. It was a Monday morning at nine o'clock, and I was due at a board meeting soon. So I hurriedly phoned Margaret and gave her the news saying that as I would be busy over the next two days; would she take it on? That was 9am on Monday. Tim was released on Wednesday, was in Gweru our home town on Thursday and was in Capetown on Sunday. Who dares to say that God does not answer prayer?

In April 1980 independence came to the country, but all it did was to introduce another enemy: corruption. Just one event will suffice to illustrate the point. Before independence we employed sixteen European farm inspectors, each with a corporation car. After independence we took on sixteen African inspectors for training purposes and gave each one a vehicle. During the seventeen years I had served in the corporation not one vehicle driven by an inspector was ever damaged. With African drivers, the sixteen vehicles given to them were either severely damaged or written off in three months. They took off good tyres, sold them and replaced them with bald tyres, the insurance company refusing to pay compensation. Even the Minister of Agriculture was not immune from such corruption. He had a BMW with an African driver. When the Minister went on an overseas business trip and was dropped off at the airport, his driver took the car to a Tribal Trust Land far from the Minister's home and, showing off, wrecked the vehicle miles from Harare.

15

Changing Careers Again

After witnessing such corruption in the AFC I took early retirement and went to Mutare to run our church there. To this day I do not know if that was the right decision. Perhaps I should have stayed and allowed my Christian principles to act like leaven in the situation. From what I gathered from a friend who took over from me I could well have run into political problems because he too resigned a short time afterwards, not being able to take the pressure of undisguised and blatant theft and corruption.

One African promoted to a senior position got away with $400,000, was sacked, went on to perform the same trick in the Cold Storage Commission, and eventually landed up in jail. Another senior man took his family on a trip to Bulawayo, stayed in an hotel and tried to make the corporation pay. He got the sack too. His favourite expression at work about the lesser mortals was that they "had no background". He himself was married to Simon Kapepwe's daughter. Kapepwe was Kenneth Kaunda's Minister of Finance in Zambia.

We went to Mutare in faith and had to sell our lovely home in Gweru. Margaret was full of hope and faith and said we would sell the house even if it meant waiting to the last day. That was prophetic talk as we signed the deed of sale on the way out of town with the car full of pets, on our way to Mutare. On the way there, we called in at Joy's home in Harare; we left the next day but left my suits behind. So I preached my first sermon in our new church without wearing a suit!

My ministry in Mutare was disappointing in terms of visible results. It was summed up by one lady saying to me about my preaching, "You are not very good at it, but at least you try." I used to love preaching, but eventually it became a burden; the anointing disappeared and my messages seemed to come from other people. Discouragement was all around, people emigrating and moving to other places.

We had a very good Christian bookshop run by a lovely American Baptist couple with delightful children. Every Tuesday at lunchtime the husband held a Bible Study at the back of the shop for local business people.

He went to America on holiday and asked me to take it over whilst he was away. This I gladly did and taught on the book of Philippians. Unknown to me the bookshop secretary, a New Zealand lady, was sitting in her office out of sight of the back room.

Part of my teaching was on the baptism of the Holy Spirit and healing. Being a Baptist she had never really heard this from a Pentecostal pastor, which I was, and she was deeply affected by the teaching. She came to our house and asked the Lord to baptise her according to the Scriptures, which He did there and then. She had a bad back which caused her to walk crookedly. She asked for prayer for healing which we gladly gave her. Nothing appeared to happen, but we taught her to confess and believe the Scriptures and not the external evidence. We taught her to confess her healing because she would be confessing God's Word and His plan for her. I would see her frequently and ask her, "Violet, what news do you have for me?" She would answer, "I am healed, I am healed!" even though her back was still crooked. One day, however, maybe a week later, she said, "I am healed, I am healed!" and her back was as straight as a die. Glory to God! She married a local businessman who refused to come to our church because he didn't like my preaching!

Another lady came to us from the Presbyterian church. Her two children were part of our youth group. She was a lovely, sincere lady, but during our discussion I realised she was not born again, nice as she was. So I asked her that if she were to die tonight and the Lord would say to her, "Why should I let you into My heaven?" what would her answer be.

She said, "Well, I have done my best. I send my children to church and I go myself sometimes. I don't drink or smoke, and I try to be a good example to them and my husband." She stopped and looked at me and then at Margaret and said, "It's not good enough, is it?" and burst into tears. We led her to a commitment to Christ and she died suddenly in a motor car accident three weeks later. She was "snatched from the fire".

After we had been there a few years we were joined by Pastor Henry Jackson who left after a couple of years to start up his own foundry business in Gweru. He was a brilliant pattern maker and set up a foundry accordingly. That was about 1985. Henry developed a tremendous teaching ministry which became, to me, one of the finest teaching ministries in the country. He had a wonderful music ministry, and it was a spiritual joy to have him lead a service. He played the organ, piano, guitar, violin, harmonica and was able to transport you out of this world into heavenly realms in an instant. Oh, for those wonderful meetings again! He had a daughter, Delia, who had a lovely worship ministry too. Even though she was only a teenager she could lead a meeting in praise and worship with maturity.

As you walked into Henry's church you would find him walking around the building playing his guitar and singing spiritual songs so that when he started the service the Spirit of the Lord was already flowing through the congregation. He would follow this with a most challenging revelation from the Word. Wonderful meetings indeed! How we miss them!

After we had been back in Gweru a few years our house was broken into and we lost a few things, but because we were security conscious we locked every door in the house and had a steel frame made to secure the bedroom section against burglars so they couldn't get into the whole house.

Henry Jackson was also burgled at the same time and five burglars got into his house before he went to bed. Two held him down on the floor with a knife to his throat, one dragged his wife Mandy around the house by her hair forcing her to open their safe whilst the other two packed up all their electrical equipment, computers, microwave, kettle, wireless and anything else they could find and loaded it all on Henry's own 'bakkie' (small truck); then they drove off. The police eventually arrested two of the intruders but they never caught the leader. Why? He was given asylum in Britain!

We brought in local preachers living in Zimbabwe and had some fine, encouraging messages from people living where 'the rubber meets the road'. No 'airy fairy' stuff but reality – coping in Christ with the current difficulties.

Believe me, African culture is different from European culture. We had a Minister's Fraternal which met monthly to discuss church and other issues. We elected a very fine young African Pastor to be chairman and another older man as vice chairman. We asked the chairman to represent us at a certain national event. At first he demurred but eventually agreed to go. At our next meeting we asked how it had gone. He said he never went. Asked to elaborate he said he had had no intention of going, but because we had pressed him and wanted to hear him say he would go he had said it to satisfy our ears!

Soon afterwards he was unable to chair the next meeting so I phoned the vice chairman and reminded him he would chair the next meeting. He flatly refused saying repeatedly as I pushed him, "I am the vice chairman! I am the vice chairman!" To him it was an honorary position not to be defiled with having to do something. Culture!

One of the outright terrorists, Edgar Tekere, lived in Mutare. After independence was declared he murdered a farmer, having a grudge against him. He was arrested and tried and was plainly guilty of murder, but the court appointed two coloured assessors who said he was still under emotional stress and let him off.

He did not like John Knight, the Anglican minister, and organised four hundred ex-terrorists to invade his cathedral in Mutare. It had something to do with the Anglican St. Augustine's Mission out at Penhalonga some ten miles away. They surrounded John in the church and pushed him up to the front. They were arguing amongst themselves as to what they should do to John when he walked out unnoticed by them. Jesus had had a similar experience walking through the crowd wanting to cast Him off the cliff. John eventually escaped to England and wrote a book of his experience and his time in the country and Mutare.

Once a month we held combined meetings in one of the larger churches. This month a minister would lead his kind of music, and next month he would preach. Each pastor's chance to preach came around about once a year. There was quite a show of unity, but some churches refused to attend, particularly the Catholics and some other mainline churches.

Every Tuesday morning we held a pastors' prayer meeting in a 'Mutare for Jesus' building, so named after a Billy Graham sponsored week of meetings attended by one of his leading preaching ministers – Pastor Thomas, a black man from America. The building was used for Christian purposes.

Snakes Alive

16

Retirement

After ten years in Mutare, we went back to Gweru and went to work for Henry Jackson and then a couple of other businesses. We ministered as itinerant preachers and teachers. The church ran what we called Short Term Bible College Courses for African pastors and elders. The course lasted three weeks with at least five teaching sessions a day. Over three weeks this amounted to a year's material for preaching and teaching at their home churches. I enjoyed teaching there and always gave them comprehensive notes of my material. As with other teachers our notes went all over southern Africa, probably to at least six countries all to the north of Zimbabwe.

In 1996 my sister and her husband, Bob, came for a visit, and we picked them up at Harare airport. We returned via the Umvuma road and half way home ran into heavy and continuous rain. Coming round a corner we saw a car stopped in the middle of my lane with a bus coming the other way travelling near the crown of the road. I couldn't get between them and had to brake hard. I was travelling too fast for the conditions, and my brakes locked. I lost control of the car, and it swerved and pirouetted in front of the bus.

We spun around, went through a ditch, up the other side, through a five strand barbed wire fence and into a ploughed field. The engine started again, and we drove up the edge of the field looking for a way out. Finding no gate we returned to our entry point and found a policeman there who parted the wire fence, and we drove back onto the main road again. It was a police car which was parked in the middle of the road. Thankfully, we drove on and then killed a vervet monkey a couple of miles further on. I didn't ask my sister for comment, neither did she offer any, but she must have thought, "They drive in funny ways in Zimbabwe!"

Bob and I took the car in for repair the next day; we were invited to return the following day and told they would fix the minor damage. Bob was most impressed, saying it would have taken six weeks to do it in his area of Wales.

I had a bit of fun with the people in the office of that garage. A few days later I went in and asked in a gruff, demanding, nasty voice who was in charge of the place. They all looked down their noses, and no-one would admit to being in authority. I then let them off the hook and explained to them what Bob had told me about the poor service he would have got in England, what an efficient firm this was and gave congratulations to everyone. Strangely enough, my joke didn't go down too well, probably because they were ashamed of their lack of response first time round.

Because of harsh, realistic facts we had to sell our lovely home. There is a story here. When we had moved to Mutare in 1980 we had sold our house and had bought a property in Mutare with the proceeds. On coming back to Gweru, we needed to buy another house. There was only one house for sale at that time; it was our old house!

We had sold it for $25,000 but nine years later had to pay $145,000 to get it back. About fifteen years later we sold it for eighty million! The value of money in Zimbabwe dollars was questionable!

After selling the house we moved into the Dutch Reformed Church (DRC) retirement village which was built in the thirties. We had to downsize drastically but we survived.

The DRC was, and still is, a wonderful church. South African in origin, it lived up to its Christian calling by providing us in Zimbabwe with much needed goodies every three months by sending from South Africa a box of necessities to every person in the complex – all for free. One lady was rejoicing greatly in her parcel because the first thing she saw was a box of matches, having run out that very morning and there being none in town. We used candles and paraffin lamps because there was little electricity.

One South African businessman gave up his job to collect the boxes of foodstuffs and groceries and drive a ten ton truck at least twelve hundred miles into Zimbabwe, delivering parcels to old people's homes right across the country. Eventually it became a monthly delivery so necessary were the provisions. He made good arrangements at the border for passing through customs so that his vehicle was not forced to be unloaded and every box opened for inspection. Originally it could take two days to get customs clearance. Because of shortages in Zimbabwe smuggling was rampant.

I do not know how it was organised in South Africa, but first of all money had to be collected from every church or money deposited in a bank account. Then someone had to do the buying. Every box contained the same goods, and there must have been more than seventy boxes on the truck. Each box had a personal name on it. The Christian commitment from the churches in South Africa to look after the poor in Zimbabwe was very real.

The complex was run by dedicated Christian men and women, particularly Attie and Anna Scheepers, brilliant dairy farmers whom I had known for more than forty years and who were members of the DRC church – dedicated Christians who saw to it that no-one suffered deprivation of any kind, even to supplying money for rent so that the Name of Jesus was honoured.

I remember one incident there. At every meal, before eating, grace was always said. I was frequently asked to minister grace but could never mutter a few meaningless words. I always acknowledged the work put in by the members of staff who had to search for food, which was always scarce, find gas when there was no electricity and search for scarce water to cook with and wash the dishes, and then, of course, the cooks who finished it all off and served us the food. When I prayed I tried to acknowledge, with gratitude to God, all these contributions. One mealtime, when I was in the middle of my discourse, a lady within touching distance slipped off her chair dead! All I can be thankful for was that she died hearing gratitude and appreciation for God's goodness sounding in her ears.

God was certainly good to us at that home. There was no water for three days, but the Lord provided. We had five twenty litre buckets which we used to catch the rain which came down abundantly during those three days. We let the first flush of rain clean the roof of dust and bird droppings and then filled the buckets under a downpipe. Last of all I would fill two five litre containers with the purest water for Margaret's kitchen.

I worked for Pastor Henry Jackson for years in his foundry. Every morning at 7am a member of staff gave a gospel message in company time. They were ordinary workers off the foundry floor. Where will you find that in the world? Each person had his own method of delivery, and the whole exercise was absolutely free of liturgy and tradition. Classical African freedom! There would be seventy workers listening every day.

Management in the foundry had a prayer meeting before going home to lunch. Business was tough and orders were slow in coming in. We were exporters to South Africa, and this was not only most profitable but earned foreign exchange so that we could buy scarce but essential material in SA. We normally sent one ten-ton truckload a month. On the very first meeting we held, Henry put it to the Lord that we would like an increase in exports, and we all agreed. At 4pm that same day we had orders for two extra loads a month! This fired up our faith, and we held a profitable position every month. While businesses were failing round and about we kept profits up.

It was a time when farms were being taken over without compensation and sometimes with great violence. The chairman, Heynie Liebenburg, had the biggest dairy herd in the country, and it was eyed jealously by many government officials. He came in early one morning and asked the prayer team to pray for him at 9am because the top government official, the Governor of the area, had called him for an interview. Heynie believed it was to discuss the taking over of his farm. So we did as we were asked, and he had an amicable interview with the farm not on the agenda.

I didn't realise it but I had a blind spot in my right eye which caused me to have an accident, so I had to stop driving. I had had my car for twenty seven years, and it was a blow to have to sell it. Soon after this I had to stop working at the age of eighty two.

The Scripture Union leader in Gweru was a Pastor Morgan Sibanda, a very fine man indeed. Because there was no food in their homes and because of fuel shortages, people at lunchtime did not go home. So

Morgan held a prayer meeting every lunchtime in the Presbyterian church on the edge of town, a five minute walk from the town centre.

I mentioned this to a farmer friend who found himself stuck in town at lunchtime. So he went to the meeting but couldn't get in as the church was packed, with Morgan every day giving a gospel message. I first heard about this on an American radio station beamed to Zimbabwe. The church held about a hundred and twenty people. I heard an African lady say on the American programme that they were able to feed on the Word of God because they had no natural food to eat. Morgan was preaching meaningful truth amidst the reality of the hour.

Walking down the street one day I met a group of girls from the church happily chatting and laughing about various things including what they had purchased. They called to me, "Pastor, Pastor, see what we have bought." They had hats, socks, scarves, mirrors, toothbrushes, soap and lollipops. One young lady was too shy to tell me what she had bought, and another whispered she had bought a pair of knickers. I was offered a lick of a lollipop which I accepted so as not to disappoint her! This was a mistake. I now had three more lollipops to sample! Then one asked me to pray for her mother who was sick; another asked for prayer for her brother who was sitting exams and needed help; another asked for prayer because she was travelling to Bulawayo the next day and wanted protection.

So we put our arms around each other's shoulders, formed a circle, bowed our heads and had a prayer meeting in the middle of the pavement. We all shared the prayer needs because I encouraged them to do so even though they had asked me to pray for them. What a lovely time we had, the ladies being so free and able to pray out loud and in public. I closed the meeting myself and encouraged them to continue in the Grace of God. Such precious people! It was natural for them to turn to God for help. Pavements were wide enough to drive a car down so it did not interfere with the flow of pedestrians. No-one was embarrassed by such an event; it was just part of everyday life. Such sincere and happy children! Such belief and acceptance that God hears and answers prayer! That's Christianity – operating where 'the rubber meets the road'. Where will you find children like that in England?

This brings to mind the time I was invited by a young African pastor to go and preach in his church one Sunday morning. It was some thirty miles away at Shurugwi. He was using a school hall since he had only just started this new church. Whilst waiting for the congregation to gather I was standing in the front of the hall, when a young African schoolgirl came and knelt down before me. She took both my hands in hers, looked me straight in the face, thanked me for coming and then said, "Let me pray for you." She prayed a lovely prayer, got up and then sat down. It was absolutely natural for her to do so – no shyness, no embarrassment, just part of her culture, to respect authority and 'sekurus' (older people). Wonderful!

A few days before we left the country, I went to have my hair cut by Rose, a coloured lady who had been cutting my hair for years. When she had finished I explained I was leaving the country in a few days and may never see her again – so could I please pray for her? She called out, "Listen, everybody! Pastor Ted wants to pray for us." Within thirty seconds there were about a dozen workers, mostly ladies, surrounding me with heads bowed and holding hands. Such a natural thing for them to do; they didn't have to be told. The Lord gave me a lovely prayer which was outside my normal way of praying, and when I had finished there was not a dry eye to be seen. I had prayed for their food supply, school fees, medical needs, financial needs, protection, and the Lord touched their hearts and mine too. Because of the Lord's obvious presence I believe He answered their needs as prayed for. Rose came and kissed me, cheeks wet with tears.

What a lovely spiritual atmosphere prevailed in Zimbabwe in those days. The Spirit was openly confessed everywhere. A lady, the wife of a lawyer, who had a successful business in town but who had decided to emigrate to Portugal, came to my office specifically to say goodbye and ask for prayer. She was not part of our church, nor were we part of their social circle, but she was part of the Body of Christ which was the most important thing. It was just natural for her to admit a need in her life which only the Lord could meet: assurance of His love and presence every day, especially during this difficult time and unknown future. How sensible!

Retirement

A father whose son was about twelve years old and was having nightmares and other problems causing sleepless nights came to me for help. After leading the boy to faith in Christ, I prayed for him and he was delivered from whatever was troubling him. He never had sleepless nights again. The father had no faith in Christ but was aware of the fact that others had faith and could help them.

A lovely African lady called Patience Ruwodo had a son who was starting junior school so she bought him a new school uniform – from head to foot. She brought the clothes to us to lay our hands on them and bless them, reasoning that he would have a better chance of doing well at school if he was wearing God-blessed clothes. Her husband, Chris, was in charge of the City Public Health Department, having been trained at Edinburgh University. He was a super chap with a lovely sense of humour. He was resistant to the gospel for years, and his wife sat in church with an empty chair beside her ready for him to occupy it. One day our pastor, Micah Mpofu, hoping to get Chris to come to a morning service, phoned him and said, "Chris, your empty chair is waiting for you in the church." Chris said, "Thanks, Pastor, I will come and collect it!" He eventually became a fine member of the Body of Christ.

One African lady with whom I did business, on hearing I was going to Australia on holiday, asked, "Please will you marry me?" (She was about twenty and I was about seventy five!)

I replied, "You know I cannot do that because I am already married."

She said that it did not matter; she would become my second wife, carry my luggage, do anything so that I would take her to Australia. African culture!

Many people with a sensitive spirit said, as they drove into town, they could sense the presence of God there. One bad character who was wealthy (it is said he made his money from brothels in Zambia), the ex-mayor but a violent man and a high official in ZANU(PF), wanted to get on the board of the local Christian school so that he could throw his weight around and intimidate all and sundry. It would have been a disaster if he had been put on the board, but if he had been at the meeting it would have been highly probable for him to get a position. However, the Lord intervened. When he was driving to the meeting which was being held to vote in a new board, he was late and was driving too fast and so was stopped by the police for speeding. He never made the meeting!

When we left the airport to leave the country we were helped by a lady member of the airport staff. We still had some Zimbabwe dollars and so Margaret gave it to her. I said that we gave it to her in the Name of Jesus and asked if we could we pray for her. She put her hands together in the prayer attitude and we prayed for her, a very receptive lady. So that was our final ministry in Zimbabwe. May the Grace of the Lord Jesus Christ and the love of God our Father prevail over those lovely people and their lovely land both now and forever more. Amen.

When we left Zimbabwe we lost our home, our furniture, our church, our fellowship, all our assets accumulated over sixty years and all our money except for a relatively small amount and finally our country which we had diligently served all that time.

But our son Brian had a prophetic word for us. When discussing our straightened financial circumstances whilst we were still in Zimbabwe he said, "Dad, you have tithed all your Christian life. God will look after you."

The truth is He has done so abundantly.

I did say I would speak more about Jack Mytton. I met a farmer in Harare whose name was John Mytton Lawrence (at least I think that his surname was Lawrence). I asked him about his name, and he told me that he was a descendent of Jack Mytton from Hindford near Whittington in Shropshire. He said that Jack Mytton was an eccentric and a reckless gambler who owed thousands of pounds in gambling debts. A wealthy Miss Lawrence agreed to pay off his debts when he married her provided he changed his name from Mytton to Lawrence. It is questionable how true this is, but what a coincidence meeting a Mytton in Harare something like two hundred years afterwards! With a name like that there must be some truth in it. I believe Jack Mytton died when he was thirty nine.

Retirement

Top: *Pip, Jack, Ann, Ted, Tom*
Bottom: *Henry Jackson, Ted, George, Peggy*

Snakes Alive

Last Word

Once I had finished recalling all these events, I had the good fortune to listen to a talking book called 'The Distant Scene' by Fred Archer. The experiences he relates were so similar to the events in my life in the thirties that I was quite encouraged. It seems that my memories were amazingly accurate.

Writing about my life has been a great joy and has brought to mind many events that had slipped into the past. Those early years in Rhodesia were challenging but marvellous for a young man seeking adventure and a new way of life.

Thinking about my moral upbringing brought home to me how my parents set me on the path to finding the Lord. My conversion changed my life, how I lived it and how I viewed the world. Events in Zimbabwe, no matter how bad, looked different through the eyes of a Christian, and the support of the Christian community helped us all to cope.

Now that we have settled in Whitely Village, Surrey, it has been a surprise to find the level of support for veterans and the visually impaired from many organisations beyond what we would have expected. This generosity and support has made our separation from Africa bearable.

Snakes Alive

Addendum

'The Distant Scene' was a delightful book to me because much of it recorded events in the thirties which mirrored my farm life as I have recorded it in my memoirs. He went into much more detail than I have done because he was constantly dealing with personalities whilst I have only dealt with myself and my family.

In chapter twenty he talks about the two churches in the village – the Anglicans and the Free Church – he himself being a Free Church-er. He remembers many different ministers and their idiosyncrasies and how the 'sabbath' was sacred to so many. One farmer's wife would let her husband buy the Sunday newspaper but he couldn't read it till Monday. The children of one farmer had to clean his boots every Saturday night but one weekend they forgot. They started cleaning them on Sunday morning, but their father caught them and shouted, "Stop, stop!" when they had only cleaned one boot. So he went to church with one clean boot and the other filthy with clay

One preacher liked to repeat the story of one young boy taken into pantry service. It was a big house, and a nobleman came to stay. The butler instructed him to take shaving water to the visitor. He was to knock on the bedroom door, and when asked who was there he was to answer, "It is the boy with your shaving water, my lord." He practised this but when the time came he got it mixed up and said, "It is the Lord, my boy, with your shaving water!"

But the best story of all was the prayer one minister prayed every Sunday night: "Lord, remember all who worship thee tonight, not only in the cathedrals, the temples, the tabernacles and fine churches throughout the length and breadth of our land, but in the chapels, little Bethels and under the canopy of the glorious heaven – in fact, in every small corner of thy great vineyard."

That needs to be prayed in every church in the world! It is beautiful and gives a sense of the goodness of God in every circumstance. This was prayed by a man recognising God's grace and mercy and love to all people at all times. I would have loved to have been under his ministry - such submission to the Word.

There was a great 'fear of God' in those days – an *awareness* of God – surely desperately missing in today's society.

One preacher, when the last hymn or benediction was being sung, would go to the entrance door and challenge the worshipers with the words, "Are you on the Lord's side?"

Although much of it was lip service, no doubt, yet there was a consciousness of God in those days. When a funeral cortege passed by in the street in my younger days, we always stood still, faced the coffin and took off our hats. Who knows what effect this had in our later years? I am glad I did it, even though the Name of Jesus was never spoken in our house.

Who is on the Lord's side?
Who is there for Me?
Who will take My Word of Love
Across the land and sea?
Then from earth a voice did say
Here I am, send me
But only if you fill my heart
With love and purity
And be my Saviour and my Lord
Throughout eternity.
And as I live from Thee within
My Saviour and my Lord
Then give me grace and also power
To shed Your love abroad
To turn all from their wicked ways
And save their souls from sin.
So that is my desire O Lord
A servant obeying Thee,
Bringing joy in every place,
That my foot shall tread for Thee
Because they see your smiling face
As you live your life through me.

Addendum

To proclaim good news to all the world
Across all lands and seas.

Pastor Ted Nicholas

I will end my story by telling of the goodness, the love and the power of God and our response to it!

A French ace-fighter pilot who fought in the Battle of Britain wrote a book of his experiences which caused him to be so successful that he was called a fighter-ace. He titled it 'Let boldness be my friend' – an apt title because that was his fighting attitude. Boldness in proclaiming God's love and compassion and authority and standards for living, and not the world's passivity, is what we need today – so obviously lacking in many churches. See what it did for him, winning the fight every day. Most of the time he forgot any niceties of aerial warfare, got close to the enemy and simply aimed his fighter plane straight at the foe and won the battle every time; otherwise he would not have lived to tell the tale. Let boldness in proclaiming the gospel of love, grace and salvation be my friend!

Wherever the new disciples went, they caused an "uproar".

Proverbs 28:1: "The righteous are as bold as a lion"

Bold means:
- Warmth of temperament
- To be confident
- To speak freely
- To be of good courage
- To dare to do
- Confidence in our own powers in Christ
- Unreservedness, freedom of utterance
- To speak without ambiguity, plainly, without figures of speech
- The absence of fear in speaking boldly
- Cheerful courage

Snakes Alive

In the book of Acts we read:

Acts	4:13:	When they saw the <u>boldness</u> of Peter....
	29:	with all <u>boldness</u> they speak
	31:	They spoke the Word of God with <u>boldness</u>
	9:27:	How Paul had preached <u>boldly</u> at Damascus
	29:	He spoke <u>boldly</u> in the Name of the Lord
	13:46:	Paul and Barnabas waxed <u>bold</u>
	14:3:	They, speaking <u>boldly</u> in the Lord
	18:26:	He began to speak <u>boldly</u> in the synagogue
	19:8:	spoke <u>boldly</u> for the space of three months
	28:31:	<u>Boldly</u> and without hindrance. (NIV)
2 Cor.	7:4:	Great is my <u>boldness</u> of speech
	10:2:	<u>Bold</u> against some
	11:21:	I am <u>bold</u> also
Eph.	3:12:	In whom we have <u>boldness</u> to speak
	6:19:	Open my mouth <u>boldly</u>
	20:	Speak <u>boldly</u> as I ought to speak
Phil.	1:20:	With all <u>boldness</u> as always
1 Tim.	3:13:	Great <u>boldness</u> in the faith
1 Thess.	2:2:	We were <u>bold</u> in our Lord to speak
Heb	10:19:	Having therefore brethren <u>boldness</u>
Phil.	11:14:	many ... are much more <u>bold</u> to speak.
Phmn.	8:	I might be much <u>bold</u> in Christ
1 John	4:17:	That we may have <u>boldness</u> in the day of

It is interesting to note how bold the enemy was against the gospel, starting riots and creating mayhem to get their message or point of view across – Paul being beaten in the Temple; Paul speaking before the barracks, before the Sanhedrin; and even forty Jews taking an oath not to eat or drink before they had killed Paul. Wicked boldness was their weapon – Peter and John put in prison; Peter escaping from prison after James was killed by Herod.

Paul was harassed wherever he went; the enemy was never afraid to show his hand, openly and violently. Wicked boldness! It did not stop Paul from making one of the boldest statements in the Bible in **1 Cor.16:22:** "If any man love not the Lord Jesus Christ, let him be cursed [Anathema]."

He speaks to the church today in the same way.

2 Cor.6:14,15. To have fellowship, to be of one accord, to have concord, the church needs boldly to say, "If you are to be effective in this world, you must be born again, born of the Spirit." It is the foundational unifying factor for the church fellowship. There cannot be a working together between churches in any locality without being born again, which brings knowledge of the Scriptures with it. Say it <u>boldly</u>.

But in Matthew 16:18 we see that the gates of hell cannot resist those in the church who are forcefully advancing against it. Let boldness be my friend.

Matt.11:12 (NIV) says, "From the days of John the Baptist until now, the kingdom of heaven has been forcefully advancing, and forceful men lay hold of it." Boldness.

There is a work ahead for us who believe.

I believe only boldness in our living, our Christ-like behaviour, our uncompromising stand for our faith, will bring the world to its senses, turn it the right way up.

When I came from Africa, my daughter-in-law, a Capetown lady, warned me not to preach as I did in Africa because "If you do, you will empty the church." I have not taken her advice. I have only one style of preaching, i.e. boldly! It is instructive to note that despite all pressures, threats, beatings and imprisonments, they never diluted the message to please their hearers. Uncompromising boldness was their lifestyle. By miracles, wonders and signs (**Acts 2:22**) God will approve our boldness.

I believe, in general, that the church has abdicated its God-given responsibility and calling. It has been given "all power" but where do we see it?

Matt.10:7,8: "And as you go, preach, heal the sick, cleanse the leper, raise the dead, cast out demons, freely you have received, freely give."

2 Timothy 4:2-4: "Preach the Word, be instant in season, out of season, reprove, rebuke, exhort, with all longsuffering and doctrine."

Are we seeing and doing this? Paul said the calling was a demonstration of Spirit and Power: Spirit of love, joy, peace, compassion, grace, goodness, salvation and beauty. The Power of the Holy Spirit over all the power of the enemy in wars and rumours of wars, Satan and all his demons of sickness, disobedience, murder, anarchy and the like. A Spirit of hope and success, victory over all the wiles of the devil, strife and every evil work. Let us live up to God's trust in us for the salvation of the world.

Britain has been at the forefront of setting up Bible Societies, sending out missionaries and printing and distributing Bibles in all major languages all over the world.

Africa and other countries are doing better than our country. Go there and experience the power and love of God daily. It's their lifestyle; they cannot live without it!

Be bold, be strong
For the Lord thy God is with thee
Be bold, be strong
For the Lord thy God is with thee
I am not afraid, no, no, no
I am not dismayed
For I am walking in faith and victory
For I am walking in faith and victory
For the Lord my God is with me.

Hallelujah! That's the message for the church in England today, so I think. Go out boldly and enforce the laws of the Kingdom in every city, town and community wherever you find them. The law of the Kingdom is <u>love</u>. Love your enemy. Love your neighbour as yourself, for God so loved the world – *no-one* is excluded – you do the same. Then God's kingdom will come. Now is the hour; now is the day of salvation!

Similar Books by the Publisher

Where Love Leads You — Ruth Stranex Deeth

When an ordinary young woman gives her life into the hands of Jesus, extraordinary things begin to happen. Suddenly she finds herself taken away from her familiar Western culture to serve a nomadic tribe living in the hills and plains of Amudat, completely oblivious of the Kenya/Uganda border. In trying to provide medical care, she faces the obstacles of superstitious beliefs and tribal politics. After a government coup in Uganda she is thrown into jail. However, each of Ruth's challenges gives her an opportunity to express the love of Christ to the people around her. It is only after she has left East Africa that she discovers the lasting impact Jesus has made through her - and sometimes in spite of her...

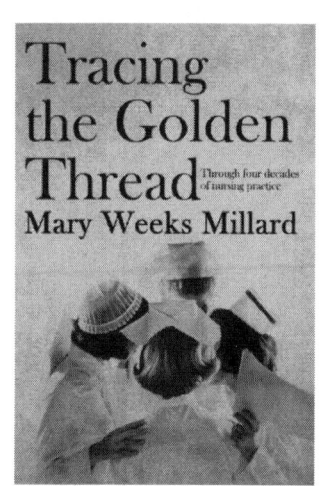

Tracing the Golden Thread — Through four decades of nursing practice — Mary Weeks Millard

An inspiring story from the frontline of practical faith in action. Mary Weeks Millard, a quiet and unassuming girl overcomes social shyness and childhood illness and a poor educational start to aspire to her heart's call to become a nurse on the mission field. She tells her own unique and inspiring life story by painting a colourful and often graphic picture of training as a nurse and midwife in the UK in the 1950s. Pressing ahead against all the odds Mary finds doors opening as she exercises her faith in a God of possibilities These doors lead her to adventures and challenges of working in East and Central Africa in the years following independence and civil war before returning to equally challenging situations in UK.' Who knows what God has in store for each one of us? If there is a burning desire within our hearts to reach out and touch the lives of others in practical and spiritual ways this story is an encouragement for us all. As life has a way of weaving and turning so Mary found that each step of her journey was already planned and prepared, offering the opportunity to touch the lives of many people abroad and back in the UK.